*"In* When Your Life Is on Fire *Erik Kolbell listens, provokes, and most of all, shares with us the enduring lessons and insights of life and faith as realized by a diverse population of thoughtful people. It's a town hall of the soul."*

—Tom Brokaw, journalist and author of *The Greatest Generation*

*"Erik Kolbell invites us to reflect on what we especially value in our lives, in the company of thirteen remarkable individuals. Their compelling life stories illuminate the richness and variety of human possibilities and the 'feast of differences' that he sets before us."*

—Sissela Bok, ethicist and author of *Common Values* and *Exploring Happiness: From Aristotle to Brain Science*

*"Life happens, and as it does we are choosing, in every moment, who to be and what to value. Erik Kolbell's wonderful new book prompts us to reflect just a little more intentionally on what we hold most dear, with lovely and unnerving examples of how in doing so we might be irrevocably changed."*

—Dr. Alison Boden, Dean of the Chapel at Princeton University

*"In this provocative book, Kolbell simply poses the question to each of thirteen individuals—what do you value above all else in your life? With a spectacular range of personalities and experiences, what emerges from their stories about themselves, their lives, and work is compelling testimony and strong affirmation of their intrinsic dignity and infinite value, the profound sacredness and meaningfulness of each of these unique, mysterious, beautiful persons."*

—Joseph J. McGowan, President of Bellarmine University

# WHEN YOUR LIFE IS ON FIRE

*To the memory of Stephanie Egnotovich*
*and to Roger Rosenblatt—*
*the brains and the brawn*

# CONTENTS

# INTRODUCTION

IMAGINE A HOUSE. A BIG HOUSE. ENORMOUS, ACTUALLY. NOW imagine that the contents of the house can be divided into two categories. First, the house contains everything you own. Your furniture, your money, your automobile, your art collection are all inside. Your photographs, diplomas, and childhood keepsakes are there as well. Ditto your books, papers, tax returns, and passports. Your baby's first shoes are there too, as is her first tooth, and her first drawing, perhaps still fixed by magnet to the refrigerator door. When I say everything, I mean *everything*.

The second category is a little more obscure. In addition to containing everything you own, the house contains everything you *are*. Your beliefs, principles, and ideas. Your personality and your prejudices. Your likes, dislikes, quirks, and brainstorms. Your foibles, fears, memories, and proudest moments. They are all there. The only things missing from this house are your family and friends (including your pets, of course, for who doesn't count pets among our most reliable friendships?).

Now that you've imagined it, imagine that it is on fire. Imagine too that the fire is so severe that you only have time to run in and rescue one item. What would it be? Maybe you'd grab that '57 T-bird you've been so lovingly restoring for the past two years. But if you rescue the car, then all the money you've saved for its restoration goes up in smoke. Then again, to shift from the material to the ethereal, if you take the money but leave behind your sense of charity, then what does that lucre profit you? It's a nettlesome question, isn't it?

But here's the deal: in deciding what you would take (and by extension, all that you'd forsake), you are declaring a kind of values hierarchy. You are saying that with the exception of loved ones, this is the thing you hold in higher regard than all of the other things—many of which you *also* hold in high regard—you could've chosen. The distinction between what you choose and what you don't might be quite fine, perhaps a close call between 1 and 1A, but it is a distinction nonetheless. To use the language of the theologian, your selection defines your ultimate object of desire and meaning. Put another way, in the vernacular of the ancient Anglicans, you are identifying the object to which you attach greatest worth, or *weorthscipe*, from which we derive the word "worship."

This is the challenge I put to the thirteen brave souls who agreed to be interviewed for this book, each of whom brought to the question equal measures of wisdom and imagination. Their answers were not only profoundly thoughtful; they were also markedly different, and as such were microcosmic indicators both of how diverse we are in what we value and how deeply those values are held. We do not *weorthscipe* lightly!

As you read their stories, I think you will see a three-pronged pattern emerge. First, you will learn why these particular people have chosen what they have chosen to pluck out of the fire, why this thing is so esteemed to them. They will define it for you, not in detached terms but in terms of its significance for them and the claim it makes upon their heart. Second, you will glean from a bit of biography how this item came to attain that significance. And third, they will point you to its universal appeal, not arguing that their object of worship should be yours, but revealing how the importance of their choice both abides and surpasses the particulars of their life situation.

Thus for instance, through the use of the elegant and (for her) spot-on metaphor of a translucent curtain, you will learn from Jane Pauley, the former host of NBC's *Today* show, that the most important thing in her life is knowing how to let the world into her life but only in calculated, digestible doses. Too little and she runs the risk of letting fear get the better of judgment and turning herself into a recluse, but too much and she risks being overwhelmed, swallowed into the great, forever-electrified maw that is modern culture. You will also learn how this sensitivity is both a means she has arrived at for managing what will be a lifelong struggle with bipolar disorder and a life-management method that makes a great deal of sense to all of us. After all, who among us cannot identify with the feeling that, like water, the abundance of the world can as easily slake our thirst for pleasure as drown us in irrelevance?

Likewise Fred Newman, a word master nonpareil and cast member of Garrison Keillor's *A Prairie Home Companion*, speaks about storytelling as perhaps the most important means he has of communicating with others. But Fred can convey that importance only partially until he grounds it in the red clay of his rural Georgia upbringing, and the role of the story as the great equalizer in an otherwise troublingly unequal South. Having done this, he makes it easy for us to understand how, from "Once upon a time . . ." to "And in that region there were shepherds out in the field, keeping watch over their flock by night . . . ," the story has the power to reveal a more nuanced truth than any history lesson, science experiment, or mathematical equation we have ever known.

Read further and you will meet a deep-eyed beauty named Regina Carter, a child of Detroit when it was still Motown, who cut her teeth on that city's progressive jazz scene and who is now an accomplished, MacArthur-honored jazz violinist in search of an elusive aesthetic she refers to simply as "the sound." You'll encounter a visual artist by the name of John Alexander, who lives for art and whose works express the love of the wild that was infused in him as a kid of the bayou. You'll read of the firefighter who aspires above all else to live the beatitudes, the nonagenarian yoga teacher whose love of optimism was fed in part by her childhood relationship with Gandhi, and the pacifist rabbi whose mission is to interpret the Scriptures for a world so greatly changed from the one that existed when those sacred texts were first penned.

You will meet these and others, each unique in what they value and why, and yet each pointing us to something of universal worth.

The theist among us might argue that this is how God comes to us, by which I mean a God made manifest through what Paul Tillich called our "object of ultimate concern" and Martin Luther referred to as that which "the heart clings to and . . . relies upon." Others will be content to observe that what we value above all else is, well, simply what we value above all else. We can have an ultimate concern and a heart-clinging reliance on it without the benefit or hindrance of a divine Other. The common thread, however, is that whether our beliefs are grounded in a transcendent theology or an immanent humanism, we are recognizing an indispensable and deeply personal, perhaps even idiosyncratic life source whence we derive, if only in part, a sense of the meaning of our existence and the purpose that this meaning invites for our lives. Whether this source has threads that stretch heavenward or is the provenance of one individual mind, and whether it is attached to something as tangible as a journal, as vague as identity, or as elusive as hope, does not finally matter. What matters is that for all of the sham and artifice that can make cynics of us all, there are things, solid things, that compel us onward. Such things are worthy of our *weorthscipe*.

Finally, I hope this book will speak to readers on three important levels. First, I hope our eyes will be opened to the broad array of ways in which we human beings find ultimate value. Second, I hope our minds are opened to the question as it pertains to our own life. And third, I can't help but think that each reader's heart will be opened by some of the extraordinary stories these people have to tell. Put another way, it is my hope that you will find *When Your Life Is on Fire* to be informative, evocative, and inspirational.

*An interviewer once asked Jean Cocteau,*
*"If your home was on fire*
*and you could save only one thing from it,*
*what would it be?"*

*Cocteau replied,*
*"I would save the fire!"*

# SEEKERS

# Chapter 1

# ARTHUR WASKOW

## *The Rabbi*

*As A. J. Muste put it, "Moses was really the
organizer of Bricklayers Union, Number 1."*
—Rabbi Arthur Waskow

RABBI ARTHUR WASKOW IS A TRUE SEEKER, AND SO WAS I WHEN I set out to meet up with him. Unlike Arthur's journey, however, mine was no great and grand spiritual pilgrimage; I literally couldn't find him. Arthur works out of a Philadelphia-based institution called the Shalom Center, a house of faith dedicated to the pursuit of peace in the world. On a balmy November day in 2010, all I was in pursuit of was the center itself. I had the address, but located as it was on a long and sinuous street where modest old homes bear a striking resemblance to one another, I just couldn't find the building. Until I did.

After walking by one front porch after another, each one in my eyes indistinguishable from the next, I came upon one that was no less indistinguishable except for the words emblazoned on the overhang:

## THIS HOME IS A NUCLEAR-FREE ZONE

*Ah*, I thought, . . . *this may be the place.* It was.

Entering a converted living room that now serves as a kind of ad hoc study/lounge/sitting/gathering area, I was immediately warmed by the surroundings. The room is lined with bookshelves, sprinkled with just a touch of appropriately agitprop art, and outfitted with the kind of overstuffed and well-worn furniture on which you want to curl up on a cold and dreary weekend afternoon. And true to its promise, as I scanned the place, checked behind the couch, peeked under the chairs and in the cupboards, there was not so much as a single nuclear weapon anywhere in sight. No ICBMs, no cruise missiles, not a single H-bomb. The place was good to its word.

I hadn't seen Arthur in over fifteen years, but that didn't stop him from greeting me with a generous bear hug made all the more fitting by the fact that he himself has a certain ursine quality about him. Arthur is a big man with a big voice, big ideas, and a big beard, none of which—though he is now seventy-seven years old—have attenuated since last we met.

I think it's the beard—a long shock of gray that reaches down a good ten inches below his chin, spreads out like an old river delta, and frames his expressive face with its craggy features and soft eyes—that gives Arthur his timeless quality. Seeing him for the first time is to be reminded of a biblical prophet, or a wizened medieval rabbi, or Santa Claus. He is as venerable as the first, as wise as the second, and as kind as the third.

So with this bearing of the ancients, it came as some surprise to me when he told me that the one thing he'd want to save from his burning building would be his computer.

"Not such a surprise, really," he tells me, with characteristic certainty, "but it'll become clear to you, I think, as we talk."

He thinks for a moment, and then adds, "I know you told me I could only rescue one item, but I would also take the ketubah [a Jewish document, used from the first century CE or earlier, that serves as a wedding contract between bride and groom] that Phyllis and I signed, and I think you'll let me get away with that because in time you'll understand how the two are bound together." Spoken like a true rabbi, whose faith lies in the belief that, as stories are told and layers of mystery are removed, The Word will gradually be made clear.

Arthur then begins to peel back the layers and reveal his story to me.

## RABBI WASKOW

In a sense Arthur was a rabbi before he knew he was a rabbi. That is to say, he has long been a teacher of the truths rooted in Holy Writ; he just didn't always realize this was what he was doing. In fact, though born into a Jewish family, Arthur didn't consider himself to be much of a Jew, let alone a leader of Jews. What he did consider himself to be, however, was an advocate for human rights whose passion was first in widespread evidence in his doctoral dissertation on one of the bleaker chapters in American history, "The 1919 Race Riots" (in Chicago, Washington, and many other cities—a long hot summer).

Thus it was that in the early 1960s, having recently earned his PhD in history from the University of Wisconsin, Arthur then began a career that, he assumed, would have all of the contours of vigorously secular political activism. He was half right.

In those seminal years Arthur's main platform was the progressive Institute for Policy Studies (IPS), a D.C.-based think tank he cofounded with, among others, the antiwar scholars Richard Barnet and Marcus Raskin. (Both Raskin and Barnet cut their teeth serving in the Kennedy administration as arms control and disarmament researchers, but were invited to leave when their views on disarmament were deemed too radical by the administration's more establishmentarian voices.)

It was at the IPS that Arthur began working in earnest as both a thinker and a doer, authoring or coauthoring works with such titles as *The Limits of Defense*, *The Worried Man's Guide to World Peace*, and *America in Hiding: The Fallout Shelter Mania*. In addition to his contributions to the study of peace and disarmament, he also penned *Running Riot*, a treatise on the roles of violence and nonviolence in the process of social change.

But during these convulsive Vietnam years, it was more than just writing about peace and justice that consumed his time and bore his imprimatur. Arthur became increasingly involved in the movement itself. He engaged in nonviolent acts of protest against the war, spoke at the first antiwar teach-in (at the University of Michigan), and at the 1964 Democratic National Convention worked closely with the Mississippi Freedom Democratic Party, an insurgent group of African-American and white Mississippians who organized to protest and overturn Mississippi's Jim Crow voting policies.

"I was very much the political activist and pretty much a nominal Jew," he told me. "Until, that is, the spring of 1968." He explains:

"Every year, despite my rather tepid affiliation with my religious roots, I would hold or attend a Passover Seder, and 1968 was no different. But it *was* different. On April 4, Martin Luther King was killed in Memphis, where he had gone to deliver a speech on behalf of African-American garbage workers. The night before he was killed, Dr. King spoke of having 'been to the mountaintop' and seen the promised land but cautioned his crowd, 'I might not get there with you.' He was both warning them of what might await him and identifying his fate with that of Moses, who of course led the ancient Israelites to the edge of the promised land but died before they entered. The entire speech had an Exodus motif to it. And with that speech, and with King's death, everything changed."

By "everything" Arthur is referring in an immediate sense to the tensions that gripped what was then his hometown of Washington and turned it into something of a low-level war zone.

"Blacks were furious, of course, and in response [President Lyndon] Johnson literally sent out the heavy artillery—the U.S. Army—to impose and maintain a dusk-to-dawn curfew on the capital. Now, although the curfew covered all citizens, it was widely understood that its purpose was to keep the blacks from engaging in a full-scale revolt.

"But what it also did was make it nearly impossible for many people living in black communities to get the everyday provisions that they needed to live on, so I became part of a group that gathered and delivered food and other supplies to those neighborhoods. But here's the thing: It's the week before Passover. One week after Dr. King's death comes the first-night Seder. As I'm going home to get ready, I'm walking past these tanks and jeeps and soldiers. It dawns on me: The tanks. The soldiers." His voice lowers to a near whisper, "*This is Pharaoh's army,*" then it rises to a stentorian shout, "The Seder was now in the streets, and the streets were in the Seder! I was never the same."

From here Arthur explains his nascent transformation by first harkening back to how he as a teacher was first a student: "I remembered working with Fannie Lou Hamer in 1964, at the Atlantic City convention of the national Democratic Party. She was leading the Mississippi Freedom Democratic Party in demanding to be seated as the real Democrats of Mississippi. And part of that was, she taught us freedom songs as we walked the boardwalk, picketing the convention." Ms. Hamer, a civil-rights activist, was also steeped in the black church experience and could recite biblical aphorisms on freedom and justice the same way preadolescent boys could recite the batting averages of their favorite ball players. It was Ms. Hamer who first uttered the now-immortalized lines about the second-class citizenship of blacks in America: "I'm sick and tired of being sick and tired."

"When we worked together, she taught us white folk a good many Negro spirituals. But she did more than that: the songs themselves made clear to us how deeply embedded they were in the exodus tradition, and how profoundly connected the black church felt to that tradition. Now, here I was, as I said, face to face with Pharaoh's army." For perhaps the first time in his life, Arthur understood that the exodus experience is not the purview of the Jews alone but also of all people who suffer from any and all manner of persecution, and that Pharaoh's army is any force that wields the chariots or tanks or jeeps, Molotov cocktails or nuclear weapons or burning crosses. Pharaoh's army is any force that in any manner—be it overt or by stealth—uses that force to subjugate or debase another people. In his own words, quoting a passage of the Passover Seder that he had never before seen as important, "Every human being in every generation must see themselves— ourselves—as moving from slavery to freedom."

Later that year (1968), Arthur was chosen to be an antiwar delegate to the Democratic National Convention in Chicago (in August), in a delegation that chose to support the presidential candidacy of Robert Kennedy. But after Kennedy was assassinated (on June 5), Arthur, having been inspired by the legacy and death of Dr. King and mindful as a historian of the political tradition of nominating "favorite sons," proposed to nominate their chair, the Rev. Channing Phillips, for president. The delegation agreed, and Phillips became the first African American to be nominated at a major party convention, receiving sixty-eight votes on the convention floor. In Phillips's words, his candidacy was meant to show "that the

Negro vote must not be taken for granted." As Arthur might put it, it also represented one more step from slavery toward freedom.

It was during this time that Arthur was beginning to feel more akin to his Jewish roots. "At one point I am sitting with the haggadah in one hand [the haggadah is the book of liturgy, read at the Seder, the Passover meal, to commemorate the exodus; there are numerous versions, but till then none had celebrated any liberation except the ancient one from Pharaoh], and in the other hand the writings of my heroes from the peace and justice movement: Thoreau, Nat Turner, Gandhi, [Rabbi Abraham] Heschel, King, and the like. So I begin to weave the two sets of writings, the ancient and the not so ancient, together into one text." This was Arthur's way of taking that original exodus story and expanding it, just as Fannie Lou Hamer's Negro spirituals had, to embrace all liberation movements, be they grounded in the events of ancient Egypt or of Memphis or Washington or Chicago.

The result of this exercise was *The Freedom Seder*, a new haggadah written by Arthur and described as "a fusion of the traditional Seder with a new song of freedom—both the freedom of people in relation to each other and the freedom of people in relation to God."

"Some of my friends thought the idea was wonderful. Some of them thought it was ridiculous: 'Nobody can write a haggadah,' they said. 'There already *is* the haggadah.' So I asked a rabbi I'd heard about, and he said to me, 'Arthur, what you're doing is midrash!' First I asked, 'What's a midrash?' and when he explained, I was hooked." Midrash, from the Hebrew word meaning "to investigate" or "to study," represents a way of unearthing the deepest meanings of the Hebrew Scriptures and applying them to modern events; with his freedom Seder, this is precisely what Arthur was doing. With this revelation, Arthur realized that he had a calling to mine the Scriptures and bring to light the universal story of liberation to which they bore witness. Arthur was a rabbi. (He was a rabbi in the purest sense of the word in that he was discerning the Scriptures for the purpose of educating others. That said, Arthur was not formally ordained until 1995, when he was brought into the rabbinate by a *beit din*, a legal body comprised, fittingly, of a Hasidic rabbi, a Conservative rabbi, a Reform rabbi, and a feminist theologian.)

*The Freedom Seder* was first published in the old political/literary magazine *Ramparts*, so word of the seder spread. The new haggadah had its debut on April 4, 1969, the third night of Passover and the first anniversary of the death of King, at a seder held in the basement of Rev. Channing Phillips's historically black church in Washington, D.C. It was attended by about eight hundred people: about half were Jews, and the rest were black or white Christians.

So to Arthur this meant that his weird idea was speaking to thousands of people. His newfound calling transformed him, in his words, "from a political activist who happened to be a Jew to a Jew who was called by Torah to be a political activist," and with the transformation came a deepened conviction to the causes he already held dear. "Suddenly," he tells me, "the words of Heschel made perfect sense to me when he said, 'Prayer is meaningless unless it is subversive.'"

Arthur continued work with the Institute for Policy Studies (IPS) for a while longer, but his erstwhile colleagues now "didn't quite know what to make of [him]" with his newfound faith perspective. During the Carter presidency, Arthur's focus on working with the emerging grassroots fellowships of spiritually creative, politically progressive Jews—rather than with the U.S. Senate—threatened to alienate some of the institute's donor base. "I came to realize," he told me, "that radical millionaires may be radical, but they're still millionaires. They like to talk with powerful people, if possible. During the Nixon years, talking to the powerful was impossible, so working to empower the powerless was OK. But when the powerful would listen once again, why bother with these odd new Jews?" And so he and the IPS parted ways.

His ministry—for this is what it now was, in spirit and in fact—then took root in a number of institutes, institutions, and grassroots organizations. Through the Public Resource Center in Washington, he worked on issues of renewable energy while simultaneously participating in a more decidedly faith-based think tank called The Churches' Center for Theology and Public Policy. Intermittently over the ensuing years, he taught courses on Judaism and liberation theology at Swarthmore College, Temple University, Vassar College, and Drew University. In the 1980s he also sat on the steering committee of an interfaith organization called Choose Peace, which was dedicated to calling attention to the dangers of the burgeoning nuclear arms race. And in 1983 he founded the Shalom Center, which brought a decidedly Jewish perspective to that arms race. In Arthur's words, the weapons buildup needed to be understood as "a modern-day Noah's flood, not of water but of fire." Since the abating of the Cold War, the center now takes that same perspective and directs its attentions to a wider array of peace, justice, and Earth-protective concerns. Twenty-seven years after its founding, Arthur is still its director.

## THE RABBI'S MIDRASH

In Judaism there is a term called "*tikkun olam*," which best translates as "repairing the world." One understanding of *tikkun olam* is the notion that, like an elegant yet shattered vase, the world is a beautiful but broken place, in which every time anyone of any faith is engaged in any good deed, it is as though one piece of the vase is restored. One small sliver of the world is made whole. By extension, if enough people were to do enough good deeds, the earth itself would be healed.

In Arthur's worldview, *tikkun olam* is a Jewish concept with a universal applicability. It is no respecter of religious sect or supremacy, no champion of one people's aspirations at the expense of someone else's, no advocate for one color or creed or nationality or economic class over another. This movement from brokenness to wholeness, from exodus to redemption— this quixotic gesture of "repairing the world" is not the responsibility of Jews alone but is Judaism's contribution to healing the world's troubles. It is the heart of his message. And it is no less urgent for Arthur today than it was over forty years ago when he first discovered his ministry.

This is why the work of the Shalom Center is so broad and variegated, and why it brings its prophetic voice to issues as diverse as the Palestinian/Israeli discord, the climate crisis, the U.S. war in Afghanistan, the hostility of some Americans to Islam as a whole, and the corrosive effects of global economic inequality. It is because in Arthur's midrash, any cause rooted in justice and tempered by mercy is a journey from Pharaoh's court to the promised land and is ipso facto the human expression of the divine will.

After explaining all this to me, Arthur pauses in reflection, staring as though into space. After a long moment's silence, he tells me: "You know, of course, that in Hebrew the word for God is YHWH. Or so we're told. This is what God said to Moses through the burning bush." After I have just been listening to him expound with such eloquence on the work of the center in the human rights arena, I now have absolutely no idea where he's going with what feels like a U-turn in the conversation. He goes on:

"In written Hebrew there are no vowels, so if you read this passage in, appropriately, the book of Exodus, this name of

God has no vowels. Not 'Yahweh,' not 'Jehovah.' It is simply spelled 'Y-H-W-H.'" Having dusted off the long-dormant synapses of my meager study of biblical Hebrew, I am not a total stranger to what he is telling me, but I still don't know where he's headed. And then, like my stumbling upon the Shalom Center itself, it is all made clear to me.

"*YyyyHhhhWwwwHhhh*. If we try to pronounce it without any vowels, what comes out but the sound of breath, and nothing more?" He demonstrates, and then adds, "Again, in Hebrew, the word for 'breath' is the same as the word for 'spirit.'"

"*Ruakh*!" I tell him gleefully. (*Ruakh* is one of maybe a dozen words I still remember thirty-two years after completing my beginner Hebrew exam in seminary. *Shalom* [peace/wholeness] is another. And *mazel tov* [good luck]. If I'm not mistaken *oy vey* [cry of dismay] is actually Yiddish, a German dialect, or in the words of the comedian Billy Crystal, "an amalgam of German and phlegm.")

"Precisely!" he answers. "God's name is not 'Yahweh.' Or 'Lord.' God's name is no name. It is simply breath. It is what we all must have to stay alive. What we animals breathe in is what the plants breathe out, and what we breathe out is what the plants breathe in. All of God's creation is complicit in this! We are always speaking God's name!"

This, I think to myself, is how Arthur can come to see his work grounded in one biblical story but applicable at all places and times, to all people. It is because, as the psalmist wrote, "The earth is the LORD's, and the fullness thereof" (Ps. 24:1 KJV). Actually, as Arthur pointed out, "The Hebrew says not LORD but YHWH." The earth belongs only to the Interbreath of Life. We all breathe the same air, speak the same divine name, depend upon that name for our very sustenance and survival. The exodus story from slavery to salvation is Israel's story. But it is ours as well.

## ARTHUR'S COMPUTER

You may remember that Arthur's spiritual switch was flipped when, after the first Freedom Seder, his friend told him that what he was doing was midrash. Since that time it could be argued that everything he's written has been, in one way or another, his midrashic commentary, and *this* explains why he would save his computer. It is because all of his writings are contained there. His computer is his scribe's scroll, his testament, his life's work. It is here that we will find the original version of the Freedom Seder, as well as such works as *The Bush Is Burning*, *Godwrestling*, *The Seasons of Our Joy*, *Down-to-Earth Judaism*, and over a dozen more books he has penned, as well as the hundreds of articles that bear his name. In synagogues the community's holy writings are contained and preserved in what is called an *aron kodesh*, a "sacred ark," normally built into the synagogue wall that faces Jerusalem. I don't know if Arthur's computer faces Jerusalem, but without a doubt it is his *aron kodesh*.

In the end it is quite simple. Arthur is a rabbi. Rabbis teach. These are his teachings. Without the teachings, he might argue, there is no Arthur.

## ARTHUR'S KETUBAH

"The Talmud teaches us that you can only acquire Torah with a companion," he tells me, "and Phyllis is my companion. Without Phyllis, no Torah. Without Torah, no midrash." I ask him to expand on this little piece of talmudic wisdom, and he does so gladly.

"If you are reading the Torah by yourself, and trying to interpret it by yourself, too much of your own self—your preconceptions and biases, your desire to have the Torah validate your prejudices—gets in the way. Only the 51 percent of you gets to talk out loud. All the other voices have to shut up. But with a companion, all sides of your own self and your companion's self get a full airing. The Torah is sublime and must be looked at from every angle imaginable, but you cannot do this alone.

"This is why Phyllis and I now write together, as coauthors. I am more poetic, and she is more structural. In this way we complement each other. Some years ago we collaborated on a book titled *A Time for Every Purpose under Heaven*," about how to find the sacred component in all cycles of life. It is, in Arthur's words, "the best book that bears [his] name." And what makes it the best book is that it bears Phyllis's name as well, without whom, in Arthur's estimation, the book would be a shadow of what it is. The midrash is now a joint endeavor, engaged in with the companion whose signature is affixed to the ketubah right next to his. So deep is their commitment to their faith and to one another that many years ago they decided to be apart from one another on the Sabbath no more than twice a year. To this day, they have kept that pledge.

We are not likely to be the authors of great books or the dispensers of great wisdom, but Arthur's task as a rabbi is no less ours. We are all called to parse the Scriptures, midrash-like, not only to mine them for the wisdom they contain but also to guard against a simplistic reading that refuses to take into account the irony, subtlety, and poetry with which their truths are dispensed. We can read the story of the exodus—with its burning bush, its ten plagues, its parting of the Red Sea—as a quaint fable whose embellishments undercut all claims to truth; or we can see it, as Arthur does, as metaphor for the fundamental human condition of slavery in search of freedom.

We can study the story of Noah's ark and dismiss it as fantasy, a kind of primitive, premillennial Sinbad. Or we can see in it, as Arthur does, as the causative relationship between hubris and self-destruction.

We can insist on the tyranny of literalism in which Scriptures must pass the litmus test of historical accuracy in order to hold any wisdom; but if we do so, we render ourselves either narrowly cynical or willfully ignorant. The cynics refuse to believe that wisdom can be communicated in metaphor, while the ignorant insist on hanging their entire faith on the wobbly pedestal of historicity and in so doing force themselves to contort logic in order to fit a pointless premise. Or we can do as Arthur and Phyllis do: put ego and self aside, apply intellectual rigor, turn the texts this way and that, look at them from every angle, live with them, listen to them, and let them speak to us not only about ancient truths but also about how those truths can be brought to bear on the most pressing issues of our time.

In the end I think this is what keeps Arthur so vital at seventy-seven. In hearing him speak about his midrash, about how he came to it, how he feels called to it, and how he and Phyllis now dispense it for the betterment of both their community and their relationship, I hear a man suffused with unquenchable enthusiasm. And that is what we all should be. Enthusiastic. *En theus*. With God.

## Questions for Discussion

1. What did Waskow mean when, during the Passover season occupation of Washington, D.C., in 1968, he referred to the troops as "Pharaoh's army"? What is the biblical reference, and what are the parallels between Pharaoh and the President of the United States?
2. Waskow quotes Heschel as saying, "Prayer is meaningless unless it is subversive." What does faith call us to subvert, and how can prayer help us to do this? Keep in

mind that we can endeavor to subvert totalitarianism, yet we can just as pointedly endeavor to subvert our own cowardice, prejudice, or indifference.

3. There is a traditional Sufi saying to the effect that "Like the divine mother who bears in her heart all of the pain of human creation, we must bear that portion of the world's pain that is entrusted to our care." How can you do this in your life?

# Chapter 2

# MARIAH BRITTON

## *The World Was with God*

> *Some barriers are real and insurmountable.*
> *But others may be of our own imagination.*
> *And 90 percent of the time, that barrier is us.*
> —Mariah Britton

## INTO THE (LITERARY) LION'S DEN

For some artists the medium of choice is oils, for others it is acrylics, for others still it is marble, wood, brass, or bronze. For Mariah Britton, artist extraordinaire and modern-day Renaissance woman, the medium is the word, be it spoken or written. She has been a poet for much of her adult life, the kind for whom the craft is so ingrained that when she speaks, she can't help but do so with tempo, cant, rhythm, and rhetorical flourish. "Eloquence is a painting of the thoughts," Pascal wrote. And so it is with Mariah: she serves up her insights as if from a palette. My interviews with her were less conversations than minirecitals whose cadences were interrupted only by the prosaic quality of my questions.

To read her résumé is to be impressed by her deeds if deprived of the elegance with which she spins the tales behind those deeds. She *is* a published poet, whose words, as Auden said of the poetry of the great Adrienne Rich, "speak quietly but do not mumble." But she is also an ordained minister in the American Baptist tradition who served for over ten years as a Youth Minister on the staff of the prestigious Riverside Church. She is a former New York City schoolteacher. She holds a PhD in human sexuality from New York University and is the founder and current director of the Moriah Institute. (A play on her own first name, *Moriah* is a biblical reference to the mountain that has come to symbolize hope in the face of hardship and doubt.) A logical extension of her long-standing commitment to the spiritual education of young people, the institute, a faith-based not-for-profit organization, helps adolescents navigate their passage from childhood to adulthood.

She is a woman of talent whose accomplishments are grounded in a hunger to learn, a ravenous curiosity about what lies just beyond our field of vision, what awaits us just around the next bend in the river. She is a worthy inheritor of the writer Muriel Rukeyser's mandate to "breathe in experience, breathe out poetry."

A tall, substantial woman with heavy-lidded eyes and rich, dark, smooth skin, Mariah is the kind of person who speaks as much with her body as with her voice, long lazy arcing arms gliding through the air, supple fingers stabbing a point or punctuating a story line. She is part orator, part conductor: the sweep of the gesture is as communicative as the content of the sentence. It is no surprise, then, when she tells me what she would pull out of the flames.

"What are the things that could be readily duplicated? I ask myself. And I rule those out right away." She tells me this as we sit around a grand dining room table in her cozy rural home. An overcast, early winter sky casts a pall over the space, which is too bad because the room—and the adjoining rooms—is redolent with colorful art, much of it of African heritage. It is like a sheathed sword. Mariah continues:

"I spent nine years writing my doctoral dissertation, but then they have a copy of that at NYU. No, I know what I would save. I would save my poetry." She pauses momentarily, looks away, then as though thinking aloud, adds in a slower and reverent cadence, every word spoken as if it has been carefully chosen, "My sense of being on the planet was strengthened when I recognized that I am a poet." She speaks these particular words, "My sense of being on the planet . . . ," as if to convey that this was an awakening that transformed her from spectator to participant in the thrum and din of the world around her.

I ask her when that "sense" came over her, when it happened that she made this transformation, and she tells me it didn't, exactly. That is, it didn't just "happen" any more than a newborn baby "happens" without a long period of gestation. No, this is an evolved recognition, an education that was gained largely outside of the classroom and seeped into her consciousness one iamb at a time. As she elaborated on this point, we recalled Madeline L'Engle's description of her conversion to Christianity as the slow move "into an intellectual acceptance of what my intuition had already known." In fact, strands of Mariah's epiphany wend their way back over thirty-five years, and yet now she is still evolving, still becoming. She then tells me of the genesis, the inception of this calling.

"I had been in college for two years, had been 'messing around' with poetry since my high school days, but in 1973 I got wind of a poetry workshop that was convening in New York City, at a restaurant called Only Child. It's closed now, but back then it used to host events like this. Poetry largely composed by African American and Caribbean American women. Some Latina, a smattering of Anglo as well."

The workshop was led by a woman who went by her first name, Fatisha, about whom Mariah remembers only that "she was one of the most brilliant women I have ever met in my life. Her understanding of language, and her commitment to truth telling was truly awesome." Pausing for effect, she tells me, drawing out her words to underscore the sincerity with which she felt them, "The whole experience literally blew . . . me . . . away!" It almost did; Fatisha's impact on Mariah was such that it nearly sent her heading for the door:

"The experience of hearing magnificent African American poetry," Mariah tells me, "made me look very critically at my own poetry." She drops the word "critically" like a throwaway, but then conveys the true depth of her doubt: "It made me ask myself, 'What world am I living in?' I was humbled."

She was humbled but fortunately not silenced, as backbone bested doubt and persistence, as Thomas Carlyle put it, revealed the strong soul. When Mariah learned that this series was going to be followed up by a lengthier program convening up in Harlem and specifically tailored to African American women, she swallowed hard, stiffened up, and signed on. It would prove to be the gateway to her epiphany.

"There were between eight and ten of us, and we met in a small room at Union Seminary. Some awesome women came through those doors. Toni Morrison had just written *The Bluest Eye* and *Sula* and came in as a guest speaker. So did [author-activist] Alexis Deveaux, Sophia Henderson Holmes . . ." Her voice trails off as she gazes out the window, into the grey, brooding heavens. "Sophia just passed on recently," she says with understated sadness and then, smiling, "It's all coming back to me now."

As it does come back, she fixes less on a moment than a mood. "These women were hard critics, of me and of each other. They didn't bite their tongues. But I believe they saw something in me that encouraged me to be there. Otherwise," as she puts it, "they wouldn't have let me hang." Meaning, she simply would not have been worth their time or energy.

Put another way, these were smart, worldly-wise women who had no patience with dabblers, and when they looked at

Mariah, self-doubt and all, they knew what world she was living in. She was no dabbler.

When I ask her what it was she suspects these seasoned writers did see in the raw rookie, she thinks a minute before she answers. Her delivery is again slow and deliberate, words spoken with caution, care, and intent. (Poets write with an extravagance of wisdom in an economy of words. This is how Mariah speaks as well.) "I believe they respected my consciousness of language and my desire to tell the story as I saw it." She tells me this, and I remind her of something she mentioned earlier in our conversation when she was describing Fatisha: the line about "her understanding of language, and her commitment to truth telling being something awesome to behold." Using the language to speak the truth; was this a theme? Was it a product of the time and place in which Mariah's awakening as a poet began to stir? She answers my question obliquely, as though we are coming up on the next bend in the river, shifting our attention from the poetry to the pew.

## POETIC JUSTICE

Her poetic aspirations were never fully distinct from the religious beliefs that would one day draw her into the ministry. In both forums she saw fit to poke at the sacred cows of prevailing orthodoxy, perhaps in search of a deeper truth that lay beneath the artifice of a world in which simple slogans were insufficient to address complex problems.

Born and raised in Harlem, "I come out of the African American religious traditions. My aunt Anna was a Holiness preacher out of the Pentecostal church," she recalls. "But in much of my early poetry, I am questioning the wisdom of God, given all that has happened in the world. There were a lot of 'whys.' You know, 'Why is there suffering?' 'Why doesn't God answer prayers?' Also a desire to have a sense of the blissfulness that the church promised but that I wasn't feeling. In other words, more talk of truth than evidence of it.

> Jesus is mine
> come to church all the time
> back pew, Sunday best preacher rollin'
> choir about hallelujahs
> send me into a frenzy
> friends play it real heavenly
> it all feels sooo good
> can't remember the words
> sermon fell apart as I walked out
> want to stay but no more to do
> preacher sleep with sistah Sue
> church deacon steals money too
> Somebody come and get me
>   —"Somebody Come and Get Me"

"Now at about the same time, people like [theologians] Delores Williams [and Karen Baker-Fletcher] were starting to develop what was called womanist theology [a theological framework that came of age in the early 1980s and was designed to reconsider classic Western religious traditions in a new light so as to empower women, especially African American women]. A language and spirit of liberation was being felt, based not on submission [to orthodoxy, or biblical literalism, or male hierarchy, or the dominance of a white culture] but on strength." Much of this spirit of liberations was coursing through the church and receiving expression in her poetry. In her words, "this eye-opening liberation was what I was being exposed to."

They were heady times indeed. "By being in this [poetry] workshop, I was then exposed to other events as well; other movements, other dynamic pieces people were trying to produce in dance, writing, and visual arts. Even though I was born and raised in Harlem, this was a new New York that was being opened to me." Her poetry became a vehicle through which she critiqued some of the religious assumptions of her youth, while the rise of feminism, particularly in the urban African American community, helped Mariah see the possibility of merging faith and creativity in a way that wasn't beholden to tired dogmas or prosaic tropes.

The opportunity to merge these two great forces in her life gained further traction for her in the late 1970s, when she met a charismatic and brilliant young seminarian by the name of Preston Washington. Washington, a poet/minister in his own right and a few years her senior, would go on to author numerous books, revive Harlem's historic Memorial Baptist Church, and establish a clergy community development consortium that would, in the late 1980s and from the poorest neighborhood in all of New York, give birth to Harlem's second great renaissance. But it was in his seminary days that he was eager to make faith relevant again to the legions of young African American women and men who, like Mariah, had long ago grown skeptical that the church had anything to offer them. He, too, was looking for truth in a world of illusion.

With Preston, Mariah's mind continued to expand in unimagined ways. "His intellect, his charisma, his questions— they all resonated with me. He not only understood that the black church had become irrelevant in the lives of young people: he also understood *why*. The church wasn't speaking to them, and he knew this. He appreciated how artistic expression could be meaningful to the young, and how a more Afrocentric view of Christianity would have appeal as well. He preached a more intellectual and less literal interpretation of Scriptures, and he linked the liberation stories of ancient Israel to the plight of African Americans." In the ancient language of the sacred texts, Washington connected the story of black America to the laments of the psalms. He likened nonviolent disobedience to Micah's call to do justice. And he drew stark parallels between the civil-rights movement and John's vision of a "new heaven and a new earth" (Rev. 21:1). "He stirred in me and in others a real sense of religious inquiry, and I found these things absolutely delicious!" Mariah tells me, a smile stretching from one ear to the other.

If Mariah wasn't yet hooked on the possible marriage of religion and art, she was at least dazzled by the bait. With Preston and other young creative types, she founded a Harlem-based fellowship called the New Life Community that met weekly for what they called "Sunday celebrations." "We intentionally did not call it worship," she told me, "because it was more of an opportunity for people to come together and talk about contemporary issues, art, poetry, politics. On occasion Scripture would come in, but through the side door." This was tactical, as they rightly assumed a prejudice among some against religious language.

Though relatively short-lived, New Life then inspired Mariah to join with other artists in founding a community called the Metamorphosis Writer's Collective. The collective published books and served as a kind of ad hoc clearinghouse for the convergence of, as she puts it, "ideas, art, and inquiries. It was a place where ideas, both religious and secular, would awaken. It was here that I met Alice Walker, one of a number of extraordinary poets who came our way. It was also through this effort that I came in touch with the Frederick Douglass Arts Workshop [also in Harlem]," where she exchanged ideas with the likes of James Baldwin, Sterling Brown, Derek Walcott, and Sonia Sanchez.

This crop of thinkers and dreamers were possessed of what Mariah called "an emerging language, an emerging voice. It was truth telling" (there's that term again). But as much of an impact as this audience had on American culture, since we are speaking with one another, I am for the moment more interested in Mariah than in James Baldwin or Sonia Sanchez, and more interested in the here and now than the there and then. So I push her to make the connection for me. I don't want to know what these bright lights of Black arts and letters taught about truth telling as much as I want to know what they taught *her* about it. She obliges, again, choosing her words with care and delivering them, adagio, with patience and pace.

"For myself, I came to learn that [truth telling] means this: Through poetry I express, to the best of my ability, the truest sense of my understanding of my life, and the truest understanding of the concerns I have for the world. It is precious to me."

Against the backdrop of a post-Vietnam, post-Watergate America, when authority was in disrepute, when old assumptions begged to be challenged and were confronted, no more vigorously than by women and people of color, Mariah heard her call to minister to those true concerns she had for the world. It was a calling that would merge her deep explorations of faith with her fundamental identity as an artist. Her theology was shaped by the emerging womanists such as Delores Williams and Katie Cannon, but also by black liberation theologians like James Cone and Cornel West, as well as Preston Washington and his pavement ministry. Her sermons became blends of poetry and prose, plumbing the depths of Holy Writ, finding the point at which the ancient text could be brought to bear on the contemporary issues of the day, where the Scripture meets the street, and treating each word, as one would expect of a poet, as though it were spun gold. "Always be a poet," wrote Baudelaire, "even in prose." As Mariah's flair for the artistic gave style to her writing, her thirst for relevance gave it substance. And along the way, in finding her voice, she landed her audience.

"As a minister I came to see myself as an educator in the broadest sense," she observes. "So it's not surprising that I have been drawn to working with young people, helping them to find creative expression for their own thoughts and feelings, tapping into their imaginations and discovering their voices." This gravitational pull may be attributable to the fact that the mind of the young is so supple and open to discovery, but it is also rooted in Mariah's own childhood, not only the days when, as a young woman, she was encouraged by the older, wiser women to speak through verse, but before that, in adolescence, when one schoolteacher in particular did the same.

## LONG LIVE THE KING

Though much of her growth as a poet is rooted in extracurricular activity, Mariah points to something of a seminal moment that occurred when she was a high school student. "I was in the tenth grade when [Dr. Martin Luther] King was assassinated. A teacher, his name was Jack Guerner, asked us to write about it. I did, and Jack saw something in my writing. He was my first encouragement. But so was the guy who ran the candy store across the street from the school, a revolutionary brother, playing jazz all the time. He introduced me to James Baldwin's *Another Country*, and after I devoured that, I begged for more. It was through this guy, whose name I don't even remember, sad to say, and through Jack that I discovered the writings of black men and women who I didn't even know existed." She read Lillian Smith's *Strange Fruit*, heard the doleful sounds of Billie Holiday, and found in John Coltrane's music the master's yearnings for a relationship with God. "We're not talking about the Temptations here!" she tells me with a smile. The poet was off and running. It is what she refers to as her "bump into the piano" moment.

## A BUMP IN THE NIGHT

The legendary Quincy Jones was not always on track to become one of America's preeminent musical composers and impresarios. When Quincy was fourteen years old, he and a bunch of friends were looking for a little trouble but not finding it; so, motivated as much by boredom as anything else, they broke into a school with the intent of burglarizing it. It was dark, and the boys didn't know the layout of the room they were in. "At one point," as Mariah tells it, "Quincy's feeling his way, and he bumps into something. He didn't know what it was, but for some reason his curiosity was aroused enough so as to make him want to return the next day and see what it was. That next day, in the light of day, was when he discovered what it was. It was a piano."

I don't know what it was about the piano that so enchanted Jones, nor does Mariah. But what we do know is that this moment marked the end of a life of desultory vandalism and the beginning of a lifelong love affair. And absent that love affair, the world might never have conferred on it the dulcet likes of "You Don't Own Me," "Gula Matari," and "Just Once," or the defiant joy of "Smackwater Jack," not to mention the innumerable arrangements, movie scores, and collaborations with which Jones has made this world sound just a little sweeter. All because, while committing a crime, he literally stumbled upon something in the dead of night that changed his life forever.

Today Mariah's work through her institute is very much reflective of her own experience as a young woman who had the good fortune to get pointed in a good direction and now wants others to do the same. The heart of the institute's work is a program called Rites of Passage, in which young people wrestle with matters germane to their emergence into early adulthood. Owing to how, in this age range, budding sexuality so profoundly colors how young people navigate the world, the program has a strong but not exclusive emphasis on the wonders, responsibilities, difficulties, and land mines attendant to this emergent force. When she conducts workshops for the program, her own past is never far behind.

"I modeled the program after that early poetry workshop [with Fatisha] in one important way," she observes. "If you are in that room, then you have something to share. And you're required to share it truthfully. Don't give us any BS. The assumption behind this is that you (the student) are of value, and what you bring to the table is of value, so don't be selling yourself cheap by telling us what you *think* we want to hear. Tell us what is in your heart. Tell the truth." The poet in search of truth. Always the truth.

When I ask her how this is brought to bear on the matter of sexuality, she tells me that she sees human sexuality, in its broadest sense, as a kind of poetry in motion. "At root it's not about the gymnastics of sex but about what it means to enter into a relationship with another human being, to learn to be friends, and to learn to trust one another. There's greater possibility in human relationship than simply doing what they think it takes to be cool. There is another language, just like poetry is another language." As she explains it, poetry is a language of mutual respect, of knowing what you want and what the other wants, and of valuing one another.

honed by the desire to connect.
not the body flexing, yearning to release
but a need to know the radiance of sharing in
the splendor that is life.

           —"Tenders of the Heart"

Mariah then takes this idea of value and expands on it. "Students and young people need to have a deeper experience of purposefulness on the planet. Purposefulness in relation to another human being, but also purposefulness as it pertains to life in general." To this end she also works with her constituency on what she calls a "life plan" in which the young person comes to understand that growth into purposeful adulthood involves a mixture of preparation and serendipity. "I was lucky to have stumbled into that poetry workshop, but prior to that I had already attuned myself to poetry. I was ready to stumble into it. I had done the work that had given me a right to be in that workshop with those women." Her poetry was her preparation, the workshop her serendipity.

see them walk right by
in front of our eyes
unread, unknown souls
teenagers, almost adult and not yet grown
beauty and potential bunched up together
all façade, masks, bravado, and loud

And we've got to go and get them.
  —"Somebody Come and Get Me"

"There's an old African proverb," she muses, "that says, 'Once you declare what you want to the world, the world brings it to you.' Once you're aware you want blue, you're not gonna take purple. You're not gonna take orange. You're gonna be aware of all things blue."

## LORD OF THE DANCE

With the wisdom of this proverb hanging in the air, we dwell in silence for a moment as the afternoon's drear further darkens the room we're sitting in. Rather than descending melancholy, though, a calm settles in on us. Perhaps, I think, the world is bringing us the color we need right now. I am thinking too about Mariah's ministry, about how difficult I always found it to work with an adolescent population (an age when impulse often gets the better of judgment) and how admirable it is that she plunges with them into these exceedingly thorny issues. I think of how, if Mariah's "blue" revolves around her poetry, then her ministry revolves around helping young people to find *their* blue, helping them declare what it is they want so that the world can bring it to them. As if on cue, she breaks the silence to offer me a story:

"A young woman in our program had been a member of a sacred dance ministry at a church where we were conducting a Rites [of Passage] weekend. The night before our program, the church honored her with an award for the ten years this young person had been with the dance group. Now to look at her, you wouldn't know she was a dancer, and I don't know how talented she is, but they honored her with this award. And I tell you, she wept. She openly wept. All because they'd recognized her. Because what she had done had purpose.

"Now, the next day, when I'm setting up chairs for the Rites program, one of our mentors comes up to me and, out of nowhere, says to me, 'I have a ticket for one young person to participate in a class with the Alvin Ailey [American Dance Theater]. Do we have someone who might want to do this?' Well of course I said yes. In fact, I said 'Yes! Yes!' And when we mentioned this to the young girl from the night before, *she didn't know who Alvin Ailey was*! Ten years of studying dance! In a historically black church! In Harlem! And she hadn't ever been introduced to *Alvin Ailey*! I was stunned, and I told her two things. First, she absolutely had to get to this performance. And second, if there was any impediment that kept her from getting there, anything whatsoever, we would remove it.

"Sooo, I think about this girl, about what she loves, and about what she hasn't been exposed to. And I say to myself, 'She goes to see Alvin Ailey, and who knows, there might just be a piano waiting for her to bump into.'"

In the spirit of the African proverb, this is Mariah, helping the young person discern, as she once did, what she most deeply desires in life. And this is Mariah, bringing it to her. She is poetry in motion. That's the truth.

❦

I think that in our search for religious truth, we sometimes overlook the artistic—in this case, the poetic—in the faith experience. I say this because the meaning of art—be it written, painted, chiseled, sewn, or sung—cannot simply be "grasped" the way, say, we grasp the meaning of a street sign or a weather report: in our laziness we want the faith message to be that obvious. Instead, with art, as with faith, we must live with the complexity, subtlety, and the need for interpretation. We must give it time and patience. Much as the mood of the art that hung in Mariah's home changed as the day darkened, we must think it, rethink it, and rethink it again as light and circumstance change around it. Only in this way do we experience the richness of the medium, and if we are not experiencing it in richness, we are not experiencing it at all.

Think, for instance, of the painting *Kiss of Judas* by the pre-Renaissance artist Giotto di Bondone, a work of art *and* a work of faith. We can give it a cursory glance and dismiss it as a dusty old reminder, one of thousands, of a lesson Sunday school kids learned when they really wished they were out doing something else. Judas was a bad guy. He sold out our Savior. Got it. Don't be a Judas. It's a street sign.

Or we can plumb its depths. A kiss. Why a kiss? Why a gesture of affection as a moment of betrayal? How does the contradiction of action and intent speak to us of the difference between the actions we engage in and the intentions behind them? How are we affected by this painting's luminous beauty when that beauty is meant to convey a story of such dark horror? Does it perhaps mean that the love of Christ is such that, in receiving this kiss, he is reminding Judas that his love for Judas transcends even this despicable act?

The point is, "the artist, as painter or poet, does not cudgel us with the obvious but beckons us to the sublime. To the depths of faith, not just its shallows. To a place where the hard questions of life, the questions of purposefulness, of relationship, of liberation, maybe the questions of God in a ghetto, can be asked," as Mariah put it, truthfully. As in her own words:

> my prayers are the bottom
> line, pageless and unsigned
> they await the right of
> all things left near the pass.
>
> a chant mounds and
> spreads evenly where
> my heart and head rest,
> silence swirls, ancient
> and sure.
> —"In awake of the coming pass"

## Questions for Discussion

1. Mentors clearly played a pivotal role in the shaping of Britton's life and the decisions she has made. Can you identify such people in your own life? Have you ever played this role for someone else? If not, how can you put yourself in a position to do so?

2. "My sense of being on the planet was strengthened when I recognized that I am a poet," Britton tells us. What do

# Chapter 3

# KENJITSU NAKAGAKI
## *Who Do People Say That I Am?*

*The vows of Buddhism help me to understand who I am,
and to bring me to a place of nonjudgment of others.*
—Kenjitsu Nakagaki

KENJITSU, A BUDDHIST PRIEST, IS THE HEAD RESIDENT MINISTER of Jodoshinshu Temple in New York City. Of Japanese heritage, Kenjitsu organized an annual interfaith peace ceremony that has, every year since 1994, commemorated the American atomic bombings of Hiroshima and Nagasaki.

Kenjitsu Nakagaki explains what he would save from his burning house:

If I could only save one thing, it would be my identity.
But when I say "identity," I don't mean identity as a Buddhist.
Or as a priest.
Or as a citizen of Japan.
I mean identity as a human being.
Because without that, I would lose any sense of compassion.

In the words of the Trappist monk Thomas Merton, "The whole idea of compassion is based on a keen awareness of the interdependence of all these living beings, which are all part of one another, and all involved in one another." Amen.

## Questions for Discussion

1. How is ego an impediment to a compassionate life? How can it be an asset?
2. How is materialism an impediment to a compassionate life? How can it be an asset?
3. How is fear an impediment to a compassionate life? How can it be an asset?

In all of these cases, draw from your own experience, either firsthand or secondhand. Don't just speak in hypotheticals.

# Artists

# Chapter 4

## ALAN ALDA
### *Reality TV Guy*

*You think you get ahold of wisdom, and then*
*you realize it's only cleverness. It's not wisdom*
*if you could put it on the side of a coffee cup.*
—Alan Alda

BY HIS OWN RECKONING ALAN ALDA'S EARLIEST RECOLLECTION
of what would become a lifetime of insatiable curiosity would
be the time he sneaked into his parent's room, parked himself
at his mother's vanity table, and treated her cosmetics cache
as a kind of Li'l Professor Chemistry Kit. It was there that
Alda gleefully, cluelessly mixed various powders and rouges
and lipsticks and ointments together, at one point tossing in
a little toothpaste "for no particular reason," all in the hopes
of generating, if not a small explosion, then at the very least a
little spark and fizzle. Alas, it was to no avail. Still, never one
to be thwarted by a setback of any magnitude, he consoled
himself by prying the back off Mom's wristwatch just to see
all the little gears, as he put it, "ticking, clicking, whirring, and
spinning." He was four years old.

Not surprising for a guy who would grow up to be one of
America's preeminent actors, Alan spent a lot of his childhood wondering, dreaming, and exploring either in his home

or amid the southern California hills that surrounded it. Happily, he's still at it, with the same boyhood joie de vivre: when I asked him what he would rescue from the fire, his answer was one that demanded exploration. And perhaps because it is coming from an actor, it has its own narrative:

"Let me tell you about something I'm writing right now," he begins. "For the past four years I've been working on a play about the life of Marie Curie, and there's a line in the play, a deceptively simple line, that really captures what I do value above all else." It is a dreary, drizzly day, and we are sitting in the book-lined study of his spacious New York apartment. The cozy room is softly lit, furnished with overstuffed chairs, and adorned with lots of family photos, the whole space just tousled enough to make a visitor feel as though he could kick his shoes off and put his feet up. The only possible disruption to our comfort, Alda warns me, would be from above, where the owners of the apartment one flight up are in the throes of a renovation. As if on cue, we're then serenaded by the staccato sounds of a jackhammer ripping into a wooden floor like a pit bull into a hambone.

Unperturbed, he waits out the racket and returns to the topic at hand, setting the scene for me of an occasion in Curie's life a few years after she was widowed. (Her husband, Pierre, was killed in 1906: in a heavy rain, he was run over by a horse-drawn cart. He was 46, Marie was 38.) "Marie had struck up a romantic relationship with a married colleague and former student by the name of Paul Langevin, but now she realizes she can't be involved with a married man. She will have to end the affair and go it alone. As she breaks the news to Langevin, he can't abide it; but in insisting that they go their separate ways, Marie quietly tells him, 'It's just reality.'"

"It's just reality," Alda repeats, just as quietly, with no emotion, no anger or defiance, no sadness or complaint to either accentuate or attenuate the mood. He pauses, long arms folded across his broad chest, looking just beyond me, as if over my left shoulder. Alda is a little dreamy, with a small smile crossing his face. Still looking past me after a few moments' silence, he muses: "The clarity of that phrase speaks to me with a lot of force. I hear it in my head when I go through a terrible disappointment, or struggle to get somewhere artistically, or when someone I care about has suffered or died. When the house is burning, I will seize that sense of reality and get out. And later I will return, to look at the charred ruins, because when it's gone, it's gone. And I will say 'It's just reality.'" He delivers this line as dispassionately as, in his mind's eye, Marie delivered it to Paul.

But what exactly is it that Alda finds so beguiling about this broadest of all philosophical categories? What does reality even mean to him? Is he reflecting Einstein's conceit that it "is merely an illusion, albeit a very persistent one"? Or at the opposite end of the theoretical spectrum, is he thinking of Iris Murdoch's somewhat disparaging belief that "in a . . . world of illusion, the great task in life is to find reality"? Or is it less a definition than a disposition, perhaps akin to Whitman's "I accept reality and dare not question it"? To answer this, he returns to Marie Curie:

"Marie devoted her life to understanding the underlying reality of nature," he tells me, and begins to paint a picture of how she and Pierre, in unlocking the secrets of the subatomic world, were the first scientists to take "the stuff of reality" and break it down into its most fundamental, physical, component parts. In order to pull this off, they had to put a premium on empirical truth. As Alda points out, "They're scientists.

"They value reality, which means they value not kidding themselves about their scientific results, or getting fooled by someone else's results. They have a powerful allegiance to reality, to discovering how things are even when that's at odds with how we would like them to be, which is what allowed them to pursue their work so effectively." A broth of Einstein with a dash of Murdoch. But it is a temperament that is not compartmentalized, not relegated to their vocation alone. As Alda points out, that same devotion to the truth applied to the much slipperier world of human relationships "is also what allows Marie to tell Langevin that they can't see each other anymore." The scientist is the one who is compelled to explore the unknown in search of truth for truth's sake, even when what she unearths is painful or disappointing. If in the course of exploration a hoped-for discovery is dead-ended, or an elaborate experiment that is years in the making spectacularly fails—"if a lifetime of research is rendered unsupportable, or a cherished faith is revealed to be mere superstition—then this is the price we pay for separating fact from fiction, truth from wish." Einstein and Murdoch, with a hint of Whitman.

So when Alda taps reality as his most revered value, what he really seems to be saying is that it is both the acceptance of what we know and a spirited inquiry into the world we don't *yet* know that he so highly regards. He didn't know what would happen when as a youngster he mixed eyeliner with blush and threw in a little Colgate Cavity Fighter for good measure, but even though it didn't unleash the pyrotechnic pinwheels he'd hoped for, at the very least he learned that if it was an explosion he sought, he would have to look elsewhere for it. In failure our illusion is dashed, but it's a worthy failure because in the dismissal of that one illusion we are also brought a little closer to the truth.

## THE WORTH OF NOT KNOWING

Curiosity implies the presence of the uncertain in the pursuit of the real—whether in a 4-year-old boy's conjectures about cosmetics, a 34-year-old scientist's exploration of radioactivity, or a 74-year-old actor's quest for creative expression—and it is when the topic of uncertainty comes up that Alda really springs to life. "Uncertainty is one of the great components of reality," he begins, adding, "We strive for certainty, through religion, fantasy, wish, and so forth, but you know, we can also embrace *un*certainty with equal vigor.

"In truth, uncertainty can be freeing, because isn't it so much easier to say 'I just don't have the answer' [and be eager to pursue it] than to concoct a structure that won't even stand up in a light wind, to support that which you wished were true?" As he poses this question, my mind wanders briefly to the literalists of religious faith, any faith, who are determined to contort both reality and common sense so as to countenance their belief only in the historical inerrancy of their particular Scripture. Not only do their arguments—conclusions in search of hypotheses—fail to "stand up in a light wind," their intransigence also blinds them to the more profound truths embedded in the stories. Alda goes on to quote his favorite physicist, Richard Feynman, who observed that "it is better not to know than to know with certainty something that is wrong."

He continues by declaring, "One of the reasons it's better not to know is because not knowing presents me with the opportunity to listen to someone else," and then explains how important "not knowing" is in his professional life:

"One of the basic foundations of acting is listening," he tells me, as, fittingly, the jackhammer chorus resumes above us, and for a moment we can't listen to anything but that. We smile resignedly and wait it out. When quiet resumes, so does he, pointing out that listening is only true listening if you are, in his words, "defenseless to what the other person is telling you." It is what the psychologist and Trappist monk Henri Nouwen called "articulate listening." Alda goes on to elaborate: "When I'm uncertain of something, and I'm listening to another person whose opinion I respect, I might just be receiving my salvation, by which I mean they might be giving me the very thing that at that moment I need to hear. . . . I don't always like to hear criticism; it might come out of the ground full of poisonous gases. But there nonetheless might be something objectively useful in it, something worth looking at." He offers me this example:

"A number of years ago I wrote a movie called *The Seduction of Joe Tynan*." (The movie, starring Alan Alda and Meryl Streep, was released in 1979.) "One night I sneaked into a screening of the film [a viewing by a select audience before release to the public]. The movie's humming along, and then suddenly, at one point, in a span of about five minutes, seventeen people got up and walked out. *Seventeen*. I counted.

"The next day, we went back and found a brief stretch of the film, a scene just before people started walking out, that just simply didn't work. So we pulled it, and no one ever walked out again." It sounded rather cut and dried, but as he finishes telling me this story, Alda is looking down, his hands clasped on his lap, his lips stretched taut. "That scene we cut out," he tells me, eyes remaining downcast, "was some of the best acting I've ever done." As I hear him say this, it dawns on me that as much as he admires Marie Curie, at the moment in which he realized he had to eliminate that scene, he no doubt felt more like Langevin when confronted with a truth as powerful as the desire that it contradicted.

In fact, as he concludes the story of Joe Tynan, he segues back to the Curie project. As our interview wends along, it has become his touchstone. "The very process of writing is a truckload of uncertainty. That's the reality, and I'm comfortable with that reality." This is perhaps because, as he labors over the Curie play, it is his sense of the woman herself that has made him more comfortable with it.

"In writing this play, I've been supported and strengthened by thinking of her as going in day after day for years, shoveling this mountain of slag in her courtyard, boiling it down in steaming pots, the steam probably giving off God-knows-what sorts of toxins, going though this grueling labor, all the while not knowing if she would get what she was after, suffering one setback after another." It was an arduous trek into uncharted territory for a single woman in a male-dominated world, with little support, unseen dangers (she would die a painful death at age 66, probably from radiation poisoning emanating from that slag), and no guarantee that the road she had chosen would lead her anywhere fruitful. "This," as Alda points out, almost reverentially, "was the very essence of uncertainty."

In trying to draw a tighter parallel between Alan's work on the play and Marie's work in the courtyard, I ask him if he, too, has suffered setbacks. He pauses as if he's about to deliver a punch line to a joke: "I'm currently on draft 48 of the script," he deadpans. Another pause, then finally adding another punch line: "And I emphasize the word *currently*." Like any good scientist, there is trial and there is error. Lots of error. Lots of effort. It's just reality.

But not only does he see uncertainty as boon rather than bane; Alda also casts a leery eye on the steely dogmatists who, at the other end of the spectrum, think they've got it all figured out. "Many have a fascinating need to insist that everybody else believe what they believe, regardless of how they got there," he observes. "It is the pernicious nature of religious 'big-T' Truth, the idea that one person has cornered the market on truth, and that if they hit me over the head with it long enough and hard enough, I will believe it too. It's just arrogance masquerading as humility, with no room for uncertainty." I recall Voltaire's admonition (attributed as well to Gide) to "cherish those who seek the truth but beware of those who find it."

"But I'd rather not hedge against the uncertainty. I'd rather accept the reality of uncertainty not only because it is inevitable but also because it is the place from where you can strike out in any direction and maybe, just maybe, find something really valuable. It is in the moment of uncertainty that we are faced with the gift of creativity. You don't know what's going to come out of it, or how you ride it, or let it ride you. You float with it or dance with it, and it will lead you places you didn't know were there but might've been there all the time." As he said on another occasion, "Uncertainty presents me with the possibility that I will come to know something I haven't known before," requiring of him "the nerve to go places that scare me, but where I find excitement and adventure."

One such scary place was, of all places, the verdant hills of Monticello, Virginia, the home of the Voltaire prodigy Thomas Jefferson, a seeker of truth who, if not roundly successful at finding it, was irrefutably dogged in pursuing it. Some years ago, Alda had been invited by the estate's curator to come down and "say a few words to a group of scholars." Only after accepting the invitation (as he put it, with typical self-deprecation, "largely because I like to hear myself talk") did it dawn on him that he possessed little more than a dilettante's knowledge of The Man of the People. Not only did he know virtually nothing about Jefferson; whatever he was going to learn before the address would probably be from books that these hearers themselves had written.

Still, never one to avoid "the places that scare" him, Alda plunged into the literature and absorbed what he could, only to realize in short order that what knowledge he had accumulated was going to be old news and thin gruel for this group. Then something propitious happened. He went to China.

It was while there on business, standing knee-deep in a rice paddy, that he met a wiry, wily biologist by the name of Yuan Long Ping. Having lived through a brutal famine, Yuan had dedicated his life to finding ways to feed his people efficiently and inexpensively. There was only one problem. As a student of the state in the early years of rigidly doctrinaire Maoism, Yuan had been forced to learn a completely fraudulent and thoroughly discredited form of biology called Lysenkoism, which could only frustrate his endeavors.

Like Curie, Yuan was dedicated to the pursuit of empirical truth at the expense of personal security. It was a dedication that soon took the form of subversion. Risking imprisonment, Yuan surreptitiously got his hands on standard biology texts, taught himself the science, and, combining a profound understanding of genetics with tools as rudimentary as ten-gauge rope and empty beer bottles, developed a method of rice production that has transformed agriculture not only in China but also all across Asia. When Alda heard Yuan's story, he knew he had his Monticello address, because, as it turns out, eighteenth-century colonial America was not totally dissimilar to twentieth-century communist China, and for every Thomas Jefferson there is a Yuan Long Ping. Here's why:

As Alda remembered from his research, Jefferson the farmer was profoundly bothered by the fact that American rice was grown in swampy, malarial lowlands at great human cost to those who harvested it (most of whom were slaves), and he wanted very much to be able to import from Italy a strain of rice that could be grown safely in the highlands. The problem he faced was Italy's unwillingness to export the crop; it was forbidden, under penalty of death, for anyone to leave the country with the unhusked rice in their possession. In the face of certain punishment if he were caught doing so, Jefferson sailed to Italy, smuggled the rice out, and did for his country's agriculture industry what Yuan would one day do for his.

As for Alda, he could now go back to Monticello and tell a bunch of really smart men and women how he finally came to understand Jefferson by meeting "this scientist [while] standing in a muddy ditch on the other side of the world." What he so deeply appreciates about the story as story is that it was his effort to satisfy his curiosity that led him down the rabbit holes of uncertainty, only to pop up halfway around the world to find what he was looking for in a place he might have least expected. His story echoes his earlier observation about salvation coming in the form of finding something he needed to know and never would've learned without first freely choosing to wander into a scary place.

But his own sine qua non moment of uncertainty, the real acid test for how willing Alda was to go places that might scare him, with the stakes higher than a risked reputation, came in the fall of 2003. "I was in a small town in Chile, taping a science show that I hosted for some years. All of a sudden one day I found myself in excruciating pain. It turns out that a portion of my intestines had gotten blocked off, and according to a local surgeon, I was a few hours this side of dead."

His condition was too advanced to allow transfer to a major medical center in Santiago, so whatever lifesaving Hail Marys were going to be attempted would be attempted here, in this little mountaintop town. "I didn't know the doctor," Alda recalls. "I didn't know the hospital. I didn't know the options. I didn't know the odds. I didn't even know the diagnosis. I just knew I might die. So given all of that, I was surprised at how calm I felt. I didn't get agitated. Instead, I did two things: I immediately accepted the reality of the situation, and having done that, I quickly dictated a letter to Arlene [his wife] and the kids. They were just some pedestrian thoughts, but that's just as well," he tells me, an ear-to-ear smile crossing his face, "because it turns out that the guy I dictated them to promptly lost the sheet of paper!"

Not only did the success of the surgery deepen Alda's appreciation for living (as he later wrote, he was essentially given a second life, a "free life," he called it, a life that "seemed to call for freshness"), the experience also made him "glad that when push came to shove [he] could accept what's what." My hunch was that going into the screening of a movie not knowing if people were going to walk out early may have seemed like small potatoes compared to going into a hospital with the distinct possibility that he wouldn't be walking out at all. There's uncertainty, and then there's *uncertainty*.

## MAKING SENSE OF IT ALL
## (OR AT LEAST SOME OF IT)

Curiosity is a means to an end, not an end in itself. It is the satisfaction of curiosity through the resolution of uncertainty that the scientist is really after in the pursuit of truth. No matter how many edits and errors, the scientist, like the actor, ultimately wants to get it, and to get it right. As Alda, a thoughtful, self-proclaimed humanist, put it apropos of Curie, "I don't know what the word 'worship' means. I can't attach a lot of practical meaning to it. But what people like Marie feel for reality, the devotion they express to understanding reality, . . . to the extent that the word 'worship' includes devotion, it's in that field."

If for Curie this meant discerning the very roots of matter, for Alda it translates into a lifelong quest to make sense of a sometimes nonsensical world. As he has pointed out elsewhere, he is the product of a burlesque-singing father who was away from home as often as not, and a schizophrenic mother who was physically present but emotionally adrift; what this meant was that for as long as he can remember, he "was looking for a rational universe" to call home. It is his estimation that if logic and meaning are to be found in life, it will not be because these things are inherent; life is fundamentally absurd and therefore meaningful only when we provide meaning. He makes this point with the following story:

Some years ago he was asked to speak to a writers' conference about how action serves as a central component in drama. Instead of giving a lecture, he had a volunteer from the audience come up and stand on one side of the stage, where Alda poured him a glass of water, about three-quarters full, and instructed him to walk to the other side of the stage. The man did so, casually, with little reaction from the audience other than a few muted titters.

Alda then came over to him and filled the glass to the brim so that there wasn't so much as "a millimeter of space between the water and the rim of the glass." He now instructed the man to walk back to the other side of the stage again, without spilling a single drop. And oh, by the way, Alda added, as if by afterthought, "I almost forgot to mention, if you spill *anything*, your entire village will die."

With the weight of the world on his shoulders (or at least the weight of a village in his hands), the man now moved fitfully, slowly, and with great care. The audience was transfixed, breathless, and utterly silent. All eyes were riveted on the rim of the glass. Time seemed to slow to a crawl. When, close to his destination, it looked as though he might spill a drop—just a drop, but enough to kill an entire village—a collective gasp went up from the audience.

But he didn't. He made it. And when he set the glass down, it was to a thunderous ovation.

What was the difference between the first trip across the stage and the second? To Alda, it is as clear as the water.

"The actions were identical, but the second time around there was the element of striving. There was something the man was trying to achieve. That is what makes the difference between a life of absurdity and a life of meaning. It is in the desire to achieve something."

Alda's own strivings (and successes) do not stop when the footlights dim; for him a meaningful life is nurtured by an indefatigable commitment to worthy causes. Not content just to entertain his fans, the many episodes he wrote for *M\*A\*S\*H* were thought-provoking, often disturbing (but usefully so) appraisals of the inhumanity of war. At the height of the Cold War, he marched and spoke out against the insanity of nuclear proliferation. He was a vocal advocate of the Equal Rights Amendment and today donates his time, talents, and treasures to such diverse programs as the Robert Kennedy Center for Justice and Human Rights, Feeding America, and Mentoring USA. All of this he does with quiet grace and as much anonymity as he can get away with. He is less likely to see meaning in life as to provide it.

Belying the allegation by the British scientist Charles Percy Snow that scientists and artists represent two irreconcilable cultures who regard each other with suspicion and disdain, Alda has also come full circle in his fascination with science. In 2001 he starred in the acclaimed Broadway play *QED*, a depiction of a day late in the life of one of Alda's heroes and a man he regards as highly as he does Marie Curie, the physicist he quoted earlier in this chapter, Richard Feynman. But now, like Chekhov—the physician turned author—in reverse, Alda has gone from depicting a scientist on stage to helping scientists depict themselves on *their* stages.

At Stony Brook University's Center for Communicating Science, Alda draws upon his training in the world of improvisation to get reticent, wonky scientists to learn how to communicate their ofttimes arcane, opaque ideas to lay audiences in ways they can both understand and, more important, care about. It is as though he's channeling a little of his father's burlesque for them, getting them to let loose, be comfortable in their own bodies, and go beyond lecturing to a place of real communicating. The academic equivalent of a seltzer shot from the lapel daisy. He wants them "to reach into the dark and pull out an answer." As he said in one interview, "Science is a great detective story, and scientists need to tell it with a passion, complete with its blind alleys and its struggles." And in the words of one of the workshop alums, "This is really hard! It makes the whole 'science thing' look pretty easy."

It *is* hard, but in Alda's mind's eye, it is also valuable because it speaks to the human need not only to discover the fundaments of nature but also to relate those discoveries in a meaningful way to others. Nor is it just the purview of the scientist, as Alda's life will so testify. It is, he would say, the responsibility of all of us—from the poet to the politician, from the king in his castle to the beggar on the street—to be curious, to wonder, to pursue truth even when the truths we discover are painful or partial or in other ways disrupt our assumptions and disturb our lives.

As we conclude our conversation, the jackhammers let out with one final hallelujah chorus above us. Alan apologizes again for the noise, but I simply shrug my shoulders. "It's just reality," I tell him. I've learned.

∽✦∽

Alan Alda is what the religious call a pilgrim and everybody else calls a seeker. In either case, he is on a quest in which the journey is at least as important as the destination. He understands that it is rarely (bordering on never) the case that the destination we set for ourselves is reached with the surety that we've no farther to go, for even when we find what we think we've been looking for, chances are that if it is as valuable as we thought it would be, it will impel us toward other roads, other questions, other goals.

For Alan, the quest is about unpacking the many rich layers of phenomena that contribute to our understanding of reality.

As my interviews with him taught me, these layers include for him at least four components:

1. The aesthetic, which he applies to his craft as an actor
2. The philosophical, with which he wrestles as he explores questions about the very nature of being
3. The psychological, through which he identifies an insatiable curiosity to understand what drives us to be who we are
4. The moral, through which, in his words, we are about the business of "making sense of a nonsensical world"

The parallels to a religious pilgrimage (by which I mean a search for meaning grounded in the belief in a transcendent Being) are striking. After all, what religion (at its best, which, let's admit it, they rarely are) does not also deal with these same phenomena even if dressed in different garb?

What religion, for instance, does not ponder questions of beauty (the aesthetic) as a manifestation of the fundamental goodness of creation, or the eternal, ineffable source of that beauty (the philosophical)? What religion does not take seriously the desire for inner peace (the psychological) as an antidote to the pervasive anxiety of the postmodern world, or the responsibility we share for the great social injustices that contribute to that anxiety (the moral)?

Whether grounded in a secular or faith-based understanding of the world, we do well to remember that the real sin may be that of certitude born of intellectual laziness, and that we are most alive when, to paraphrase the Gospel according to John, it is with heart, mind, soul, and strength that we are in pursuit of the good. Or in the words of the decidedly earthier Simone de Beauvoir, "I tore myself away from the safe comfort of certainties through my love for truth—and truth rewarded me."

## Questions for Discussion

1. Reflect on the tension between resignation and grief that may have been present in Marie Curie's life when she decided to end the relationship with Langevin. Does her acceptance of "It's just reality" preclude emotional protest on her part?

2. "We strive for certainty," Alda says, "but you know, we can also embrace uncertainty with equal vigor." What is the appeal of certainty, and how can its pursuit limit us? Conversely, what is our fear of uncertainty, and how can a "vigorous embrace" of it enrich our lives?

3. How do you think Alda's humanism has shaped and informed his humanitarianism?

# Chapter 5

# JOHN ALEXANDER
## *The Poet with a Paintbrush*

*John Alexander, skilled draftsman and sharp-eyed artist,
has spent a career rendering "the dark side of man,
the glorious side of nature, and the destruction of both."*
—Ann Landi, *Art News*

AS WITH MOST ARTISTS' WORKS, TO LOOK AT THE PAINTINGS OF John Alexander is to be given a glimpse into much about both how and what the man thinks and feels; his history, his predilections, his tastes, his biases, his values, his roots. Even his favorite colors. From the profound to the mundane, artists cannot simultaneously hide themselves from us and be true to their calling: John Alexander, a lithe, fit man with lissome hands, a winsome smile, and a subtle, self-deprecating wit, is true to his calling. John, who makes his living—and, along with his wife and son, his home—in New York City (the art world equivalent of a mixed martial arts arena), not only tolerates the scrutiny that comes with his self-revelatory works; he also revels in it.

Take for instance his frenetic, high-wattage *I've Been Living in a Hydrogen Bomb*, a 22-foot-long, 12-foot-tall behemoth of expressionist energy held tight, like Picasso's rambunctious *Guernica*, only by the constraints of the rectangular canvas.

The painting is ablaze with fiery streaks of gold punctuated with dark shades and overlaid with hundreds of scratches and squiggles moving in every direction. Since Alexander created it at a time of great dislocation in his life, *Hydrogen Bomb* is a meditation on John's own psychological and situational turmoil. Rather than allow that turmoil to be spoken—if at all— with a suppressed, muted murmur, John ventures large as if to tell us how our greatest vulnerabilities must be met with our highest degree of valor. As he dryly observed to one reviewer, "I guess it was a form of exorcism that kept me from becoming an ax murderer."

By comparison, his beautifully moody *Roscoe,* an understated landscape rendering of a bay in the small gulf town of that name, is reflective of John's Texas upbringing and the grasp that the backcountry always held on him, just as his apocalyptic *Cry Me a River* hints at the encroachment of so-called civilization that he sees as a kind of Damoclean sword hanging low over that bay and places like it. "I love being in nature, and I mourn while watching geese flying with nowhere to land," he tells me. "Nothing but Home Depots, Costcos, Hooters. For me, birds' losing their habitat is a metaphor of the world's losing art. Whoever said 'art imitates life' [it was Aristotle] had it right. And I don't have optimism about the future."

John's pessimism is evenly divided between nature *and* art, two passions that are inextricably bound together in his history and therefore in his consciousness. Having been born and reared in Beaumont, Texas, and Wetumpka, Alabama, John is a product of the Gulf of Mexico and its uniquely brooding bayou geography. Not surprisingly, one of his earliest works, *Pasinger Boat (sic)* was likely inspired by his frequent boyhood trips to the docks and the constant thrum of activity he witnessed there. Also not surprising is the fact that he rendered it in 1951, when he was five years old. John is an artist no less surely, no less enduringly, no less genetically than he is a child of that bayou. So perhaps this is why his object of rescue from the burning home would be his ability to create art. It is not because he apprises his talent as a thing to be held in high esteem—indeed, compared to critics he is positively self-effacing about his work—but because it is as much a part of him as the food that he eats and the air that he breathes. In his own words, John Alexander "cannot not create art." More than merely his oeuvre, it is his core.

"I've never taken more than three weeks off from art without it turning me into a complete wreck," he confesses in a Texas twang still resolute even after forty years' living in the northeast. "My entire identity, going all the way back to Davy Crockett Junior High School in Beaumont, Texas, is as an artist." It has become, for him, like the goose's habitat, an endangered homeland.

## ART AS IT SHOULD BE: THE GOSPEL ACCORDING TO JOHN

Fundamental to John's understanding of art is his understanding of what humanity requires of us: that we be honest. John has no patience with duplicity. "I struggle with the idea of staying pure and doing what I want to do in terms of my paintings," he muses. "I paint swamps, bayous, crazy Creole demonic creatures, because that is how I see the world around me. It's honest, if not popular." Echoing his edict that he cannot not do art, he cannot abide artifice for the sake of status. And it's this schism between honesty and popularity that so troubles him.

His opinions about this divide are fiercely held and poetically spoken: "The art world has become a cruel and shallow money pit," he tells me, eyes downcast in melancholic reflection, "where pimps and thieves run free and the weak die like dogs. . . . At its worst, it's a collection of people who see this business as an opportunity to make money; it's shameless self-promotion and greed.

"Let me give you an example. A woman can paint a portrait of herself on a big canvas, and it can have no artistic merit, but if she portrays nothing more on that canvas than her [genitalia], somebody will be able to sell it for a lot of money and call it art. Now, compare that to . . ." He thinks for a minute. "Compare it to the very last Rembrandt self-portrait. [Rembrandt was reputed to have done over 70 self-portraits throughout his life.] In this last painting we see a broken old man. His wife has died, his daughter has died, his career has died. There is a deep and abiding sadness to this work. It pained people to look at it. Certainly no one wanted to *buy* it." John's voice is strong but cracking, as if he is revisiting an old psychic wound. Then sadness turns, however subtly, to contempt.

"But he wasn't doing [this painting] to get a show in some fancy downtown gallery; he was doing it because of a deep need. The man had lived a full life, an interesting life, and here as always he needed to be *honest* about reflecting that life." It is John's anguish that the study of, not nudity, but "gratuitous nudity with no artistic merit" would find greater acceptance and wider audience in today's art world than the pathos of this fallen king in the winter of his years.

From his lament over what that world has become, he turns his thoughts to what it was, and herein lie the seeds of his discontent. It is not just that he sees rampant commercialization compensating for a lack of conviction and mediocre talent; it is also that it wasn't always like this. There was once a greatness to the profession. "Maybe I'm just an old guy, an army of one," he begins. "But it troubles me, because I have such a deep appreciation for the history of art. Look back at ancient Egypt, Greece, and Rome. Look at Tibet, India, China. Look at the frescoes of Siena and Assisi; come up through the

American luminous paintings of the Hudson River school. In all of these you'll find great skill in organization and composition, in understanding tonality and color.

"The great ones," he adds, "were people who had an ability to take the world around them and reorganize it in their own thought process," and in so doing "create something that has a real effect on fellow human beings, touching them in a way that made them smile or think or feel an emotion." He speaks in the tone of a man who is protecting the best of his profession with a ferocity with which he would protect his very life.

John then considers his dilemma from the standpoint of a more recent experience: "The other day I was looking at some etchings Otto Dix did during the First World War. [Dix, a German artist, depicted the brutality and spiritual desolation of modern warfare.] There's nothing whatsoever beautiful or even attractive about them, but they're powerful, intense, thought provoking. And so they accomplish what great art is supposed to accomplish, no less so than does, say, a Monet sunset." Whether it is Dix's rawness or, at the opposite end of the atmospheric spectrum, Monet's gentility, each succeeds because each is, in John's estimation, "an honest assessment of the artist's thought process and how they use their talent to produce something both profound and lasting.

"You can't make great literature or music if you can't write a sentence or play harmony. A ten-year-old child pounding the piano with his fist does not constitute a musician. But in my profession you don't seem to need talent to reach superstardom, and that's troubling me." Returning to the esteem he places on honesty, John adds, "It's not art; it's a trick."

In an unguarded moment John lets me know that though the battle is pitched, he does not really believe himself to be an army of one. "My gripe isn't with the artists who deeply care about the creative process and then make beautiful, wonderful, provocative things." And he knows those folks are out there, but the problem is that he fears their presence is being eclipsed by, as he puts it in unadorned vernacular, "the bombastic self-promoters who can drop a little shit in a porcelain bowl, put the bowl in the corner of a museum [the Italian conceptual artist Piero Manzoni actually pulled this stunt] and call it great sculpture." Then, as he again puzzles over this contradiction between art and hustle, between honesty and prevarication, between the creative processors and the self-promoters, he adds, hopefully, "Look at the best paintings of Chuck Close [a photorealist of unparalleled talent, and a contemporary and friend of Alexander]. Chuck is the consummate serious artist. The best of Chuck Close," he tells me, with real reverence in his voice, "is absolutely beautiful, breathtaking, and powerful art." As the art critic John Haber observed, "Close dares to stake his humanity on his art, his art on mechanical reproduction, and its reproducibility on his fallible humanity." To which Alexander adds, reverence giving way to just a hint of tranquility, "As long as there are Chuck Closes out there, maybe we'll be alright."

## ROOTS: GIMME THAT OLD-TIME RELIGION

It would be easy to dismiss John's screeds as sour grapes: jealousy camouflaged as integrity from a guy whose recourse for having missed out on the big bucks is to put in his crosshairs a younger crowd of artists who cashed in by selling out. And though it would be easy, it couldn't be further from the truth. In fact, John has enjoyed enormous success throughout his career and continues to do so today. His works have hung in prestigious galleries worldwide, from New York's Marlborough Gallery, to the Read Gallery in Johannesburg, to Galerie Herve Odermatt in Paris. "Alexanders" can be found in the permanent collection of the Corcoran Gallery in Washington, D.C., and the Dallas Museum of Art as well as the Metropolitan Museum of Art in New York. And in 2010 major one-man retrospectives of his work were launched at both the Museum of Fine Arts in Houston and the Smithsonian American Art Museum in Washington. For over forty years, John has been well regarded, well received, and well compensated. He has made a living if not a fortune doing this thing that he cannot not do.

No, his is not a loser's rant but a lover's quarrel, stemming from what he sees as a kind of vocational infidelity. His partnership with art was grounded in the quid pro quo notion that the artist would bring talent, heart, and courage to bear on the canvas, and that the art world would in return allow itself to be emotionally stirred and intellectually provoked by its experience of that canvas. The rub, though, is that over time his partner has reneged on its vows, and where they once wanted aesthetic, in his estimation they now settle for sensationalism. It is less that John is angry than that he is heartbroken over his relationship to this vocation that he cannot not love, this one thing he would have no choice but to rescue from a burning building, and it leaves him uncertain about its future. As he points out, in comparison to his own career arc, "I've been lucky [with my career]; but there's a sense of unfairness, especially for good young artists. Galleries are closing, and many won't take chances on unknowns, despite the promise they may show."

To understand the depths of John's anguish, one must first understand the roots of his impatience with dishonesty. By his own reckoning, they are in the church. Specifically, the conservative upper-crust white church of the deep South in the 1950s.

In a town and a time when religion meant everything, John recalls the Baptist church of Beaumont, Texas, the church his mother dutifully hauled his sin-scarred soul off to every Sunday, as a focal point in his development, a place low on joy and high on judgment. "We'd go to our all-white church with its big cars parked in the lot, and we'd sing, 'Red and yellow, black and white, all are precious in his sight, Jesus loves the little children of the world.' But I tell ya, that congregation would have absolutely gasped if a black man walked into that sanctuary. Unless he was carrying a broom."

Nor was it just the hymns that spoke to what was, in his eyes, the dishonesty of worshiping an inclusive God in an exclusive enclave. "I remember how the sermons always seemed to be about how screwed up everyone is. Well, for my money, if you tell a child over and over again how ugly he is, he's gonna think he's ugly. And if you tell a congregation how fucked up things are and use scare tactics about fire and brimstone, hell and damnation, and how they shouldn't dance, shouldn't listen to rock music, shouldn't drink, shouldn't have sex, how the only people who want to integrate the schools are godless communists, well, they're gonna believe that too.

"We'd go through this every Sunday, and I'd say to myself, 'Where is the joy?' And then everyone would get back into those nice cars and drive to their ranch homes and their high-paying jobs with the oil companies. But there was no joy."

John somehow sensed that if there *was* joy to be found in religion, it would have to be found elsewhere. And it was. "My friends and I would walk by the little storefront churches where the black community worshiped, and we'd hear this glorious music. We'd look inside and see the people truly celebrating. And sometimes we'd worship with them. And you know what? We were always welcomed."

It puzzled John, and he would wonder, "Why [is there] so much joy coming out of this place where people live such horrible lives, dwelling in dirt-floored homes, picking cotton for cruel masters, being denied the right to sit at a lunch counter let alone the right to vote—remember, this is still the 1950s in the deep South—while up the street at Beaumont Baptist, religion made the folks of means so incurably miserable?"

But beyond puzzling him, this cultural schizophrenia that he witnessed most vividly in his youth—the exultancy of the poor despite their poverty, over against the languor of the wealthy despite their wealth—would infuse his work for years to come. His canvases are redolent with dichotomies that bespeak the artist's preoccupation with a divided, paradoxical, and broken world.

Through the use of warm, dark, earth-toned colors overlaid with an abundance of jagged linearity, John sets out to provide the observer with a keen sense of motion, often frenetic and suggestive of these divisions, depicting a world (and an artist) in tumult or even on the verge of Armageddon. The symbolic figures he presents—lovers in flaming masks, predators and prey, fat cats and skeletons—are often ill-suited to be in the same space together except for the fact that in their uneasy proximity to one another, they generate even greater sparks. In a close inspection of a work such as his *Annunciation*, for instance, we see images of black men in chains but ascendant, reminiscent of the stubborn, paradoxical hope that sprang from those storefront churches he saw as a child, just as in the center of his much more cataclysmic, Bosch-like *Parade* (inspired by James Ensor's *Christ's Entry into Brussels in 1889*), one's eyes fall on the overweight, well-dressed business executive with a look of drear on his face, a halo around his head, and an outsized dollar bill in his hand.

Not surprisingly, given the pervasive influence of the church in the 1950s Texas culture and the unsettling encounters John had with it, his expression of this clamorous world redounds with religious imagery and themes. Reminiscent of the stark differences he saw between the authenticity of the black church and the artifice of the white, and of that duality being emblematic of the more pervasive duality he saw in the general culture, we also find in *Parade* what appear to be kings, Klansmen, and charlatans all donning showy crosses, while in another, the *Little Prince Prohibited from Polishing His Crown*, we come face-to-face with the dark, almost-sepulchral image of a black man hung, cruciform, crown on his head, in what suggests a swampland lynching. Elsewhere and in less literal and more tacit ways, we encounter in John's works contrasting, sometimes secularized, but nonetheless classical theological themes of sin and redemption, hope and despair, damnation and salvation, alienation and reconciliation. John has gladly left the church, but by his own admission the best of it is never far from his passions.

## NATURAL TO THE CORE

These days the place those passions seem to receive broadest expression is in nature and in John's depiction of the natural world, as he sees it, as he remembers it, and as he frets over its future. Nature has become his altar, his sanctuary, his Eden before the fall. When he speaks of it, he is positively elegiac. "In nature," he muses, "there is a quiet that is so conducive to my working as an artist."

His is a wide swath cut through the natural environment. In great seascapes and landscapes, in renderings of mighty beasts such as crocodiles and simians, John communicates his reverence for the power that inheres in nature. "I look at a storm coming across Montauk [Montauk Point is at the eastern tip of Long Island, where the island gives way to the Atlantic Ocean], the orange, the crimson at sunset, the iridescent green seas, diving birds," he says, a faraway look in his glistening eye. "I take all this in, and I say to myself, this is *truly* something. I am truly inspired by visual impact."

And if he is not depicting nature's grandeur, it may be her sheer fecundity. "When I think of my childhood along the Texas and Louisiana coast, I think of the bayous and their clear, dark water. Cyprus trees, mist, fog. Swamp, with its frogs and herons, alligators, snakes, fish, owl, bugs, crickets. The noises, the smells, the feel. That," he says with particular emphasis, "that, as a child, was my gothic cathedral. And the force of that imagery still drives me today." It is imagery that surfaces in the many, many wetlands oils he has created over the years.

While his paintings of nature lack the bite and social satire of much of his other work, it does not mean they are without power. It is a power that speaks for itself, even when it is not conveying nature's great heft, even when it is conveying her delicacy. His portrait of a cluster of lotus flowers suggests both the subject's extreme durability and its fragility, just as his pastel *Great White Heron*, with the bird standing steady, alone, and on alert in the spongy fen, displays its beauty but also its staunch dignity.

As early as 1975, while he was living in a Houston that was undergoing untrammeled expansion at nature's expense, John displayed his growing concern about the future of that fragile environment as it met the headwinds of human encroachment, infusing his landscapes with what one critic aptly called the "disconcerting psychological punch" of emptiness and debris. Some years later in an evocative work called *Glory Bound*, he depicted a steam locomotive emerging from a jungle thicket, a reminiscence of his East Texas boyhood and a symbol of that encroachment of industrial progress into the natural world. Sounding a hopeful note, another critic called John's musings on the collisions between the natural and the made world his "hymn to the earth—idylls of a lonesome landscape, which will survive our concrete girding."

But whether John's depictions of his love affair with nature augurs a brighter future—or for that matter, whether his paintings are even meant to urge such optimism—is in final analysis an unanswerable question. The *Great White Heron* is, by all indications, safe and very much unmolested in its soggy habitat, with not so much as a wisp of human interference anywhere to be seen. But then again, there were those geese, flying overhead, looking in vain for last year's breeding grounds that have become this year's strip mall.

And so we are left to ponder the vast schism between that which is truly good in the world and the corruptibility of that goodness. Eden *after* the fall. In the eyes of the artist, faith that asks the hard questions without the pretense of easy answers must compete with the prosperity-pimp preachers who guarantee salvation to anyone who embraces their notion of a petty, parochial, and vindictive little god. The gut-wrenching honesty of a Rembrandt self-portrait must stand in stark contrast to the banality of the so-called hipster artist whose nimbleness is evinced only in her talent for self-promotion. And the primeval hallelujah chorus, the barks and tweets and roars and trumpets and trills, sung in full-throated unison by the birds of the air and the beasts of the field—this chorus of nature must strain to be heard above the roar of the locomotive that has come uninvited to strip their home of its wood and food and minerals.

I don't know if art will endure over commerce, or if integrity will trump opportunism. I don't know if the geese will find a place to alight and call it home, and I don't know if the artist will rediscover among his peers the rare alchemy of vision and discipline and call *it* home. But as John tells me his story, riddled as it is with plaint and pessimism, I am given to hope. There are two reasons for this.

The first pours forth from the pure passion of the man who cannot not do art. Like Chuck Close, he is a steady master of his canvas; and like Rembrandt, he paints what he must to purge his soul rather than to fatten his wallet. And like both, his is a self-definition that is not peripheral but intrinsic. In his own words, art is his "core identity: a belief in the importance and power of image making that is intrinsic to every culture." In this sense he is a keeper of a flickering flame, the culture's conscience. His responsibility is to make art, but not only to scratch his own creative itch or to put food on his table. It is to tell the story of his culture, as artists have always done. And I think this drives his passion as well. We have always had story-tellers, and we always will. So perhaps this does augur hope.

The second grows out of a story John told me as we neared the end of one of our conversations. In the telling of the story, what he lacked in details he more than made up for in sentiment: "I remember going to a giant, gothic cathedral. It was somewhere in Europe; I don't know where, and I don't remember when. But it was a huge place, in what was once countryside." As he says the word "huge," his eyes look up, and his right hand issues a broad upward sweep, as if to suggest great buttresses rising high above us.

"Inside the cathedral were candles everywhere, and they were all burning. There were brilliant frescoes, beautiful stained-glass windows, and a grand pipe organ. It was one of those days when the light was just right, and it seemed to be pouring in everywhere."

He pauses a minute, reflecting, I suspect, on what it was like to have been in that space at that time. Then he continued: "I thought back to when the cathedral was new, hundreds of years ago, and what it must've been like for a peasant, who lived an impoverished life, to have walked across those tilled fields, walked through the dirt that symbolized both his livelihood and his station in life, and stepped into that space. It must've been joy beyond words. And, like religion, this is the goal of the artist. It is to bring us to euphoria." And for a moment John is not speaking of a religion of joyless damnation, nor is he himself joyless, damning his vocation.

It is a story that contains all of the elements close to John's soul. There is the transcendent glory of the aesthetic, symbolized musically in the organ and visually in the artwork. There is the reverence we must have for the natural world, symbolized in the streaming sun and the earth beneath the peasant's feet. There is religion at its best, symbolized in the transformative power of the building itself. And there is the purity of humankind, symbolized in those who, though low of stature, could enter a holy place and, no less so than anyone of higher station, could feel that they were in the presence of the divine.

∞≫∞

Viewed through the eyes of the aesthete, John's story is one of art; but from the perspective of the theologian, it is one of calling, calling being defined as that to which we feel inexorably and divinely summoned. It is the place where our doing and our being come together, become one: God's plan and purpose for us. John doesn't just *make* art: he *is* an artist.

It is a deeply held belief in many faiths that God invites us not just to withstand life but also to live it rich in purpose; if we subscribe to this belief, it is our responsibility to ascertain what that purpose is and how best to pursue it. What are our passions and predilections, our gifts and delights? How can they be put to use in ways that enhance our sense of meaning, our gratitude for living, and in some manner—however obvious or obliquely—add worth to the world?

We need not conflate calling with vocation, since they are not always the same thing. Consider some who gave their lives to righteous pursuits but who made their livings elsewhere: St. Cyprian taught rhetoric, St. Luke was a physician. Margaret of Antioch was a shepherd, and Matthew was a tax collector. John Alexander could have dug ditches to pay the rent, but his calling would still have been to art because it is the thing that courses through his veins, the merger of his talent with his temperament. Vocation is that which makes us feel fully alive; it is what defines a life that is valued rather than squandered. It marks our place in the divine creation, the place that God has intended for us to be. We may be but a brushstroke on the great canvas, but absent that stroke, the canvas would be just a little dulled now, wouldn't it?

## Questions for Discussion

1. "I struggle with the idea of staying pure and doing what I want to do in terms of my paintings," John says. Have you ever found yourself in a situation where you were tempted to sacrifice honesty in the name of popularity?

2. Can any form of art hold the power to be transcendent, revealing of a higher power, transporting to another plane? Or is this just the purview of religious art?

3. "It's important to understand," wrote Gabriel Wilson, "that at every point of opposition to who we are or to what God has called us to do, we are presented with the options of either conforming and giving in, or standing our ground and becoming stronger in who God has made us to be." What is your calling, and how did you discover it? What makes it a calling rather than simply a means of employment, activity, or busyness (however generous or meaningful)?

# Chapter 6

# REGINA CARTER

## *The Sacred Sound*

*When performing, there are times when the ecstatic happens.*
—Regina Carter

## A MORE THAN THEORETICAL QUESTION

If there was one thread that worked its way through each conversation I had about what a person might rescue from the burning building, it was that everyone thought long and hard before answering me. Some people needed days, and others took weeks before coming up with an answer that satisfied them. Everyone took the question and turned it over, this way and that, long and hard. Everyone, that is, except Regina Carter, jazz violinist of impeccable repute, international renown, irrefutable force, and irresistible charm. Leave it to a jazz impresario to wing it. With Regina, the answer was less reflection than reflex:

"So, Regina, imagine your home is on fire and you can rescue just one item. What would it . . ."

"MY VIOLIN!"

". . . be?"

A big, broad grin crosses her face before she breaks out into a kind of contagious, full-body laughter, only to then apologize, needlessly, for her haste. Regina is a bright, tiny woman with high-beam eyes and an even brighter personality. A dreadlocked beauty, she exudes the same charm I first saw and heard in her over twenty-five years ago at Michigan's Oakland University, where she was an undergraduate music major and I was a campus minister. After a quarter century hiatus, both having gravitated to the New York City environs, we are now sitting across from one another in my living room, engaged either in an interview punctuated by reminiscences, or a reminiscence punctuated by interview. I'm not sure which. She continues:

"You see, it just so happens I was on the road last week. The fire alarm went off in the hotel, and we were ordered to evacuate, in the middle of the night! Without thinking, I just grabbed my violin. Nothing else. Just my violin. And ran for the exit. In my pajamas. So I guess it's more than a theoretical exercise for me, isn't it?"

## AWAKE, AWAKE TO LOVE AND WORK

When Regina told me her violin was her most valued object, I sort of half expected her to launch into one of those poetic rhapsodies an adolescent boy might go into about his first car. I thought I might hear about the emotional and perhaps even spiritual connection between artist and implement, about how, when she plays, she can't differentiate between where the instrument ends and the musician begins, or about how she imbues it with anthropomorphic or even totemic qualities.

But in Regina's case the more appropriate metaphor is less the kid's hot set of wheels, and more the day laborer's trusted pickup; a tool of the trade. Dependable, not an end in itself, but a means to an end. Not bliss but the vehicle that transports her to that bliss. Indispensable to the journey but not to be confused with the destination

"The violin I have now is the third one I've owned. It supposedly dates from the late 1800s, but it's had several parts replaced. I call it my Kmart special," she says, with a giggle. She goes on to explain how, as much as she values the instrument, their relationship with one another is strictly utilitarian. It is a business partnership rather than a love affair.

"It's a tool," she tells me. "The instrument *doesn't* soothe my soul, it *isn't* a romantic connection," she adds, emphasizing the negative as if she knew preemptively what I was expecting to hear and thought it wise to disabuse me of it posthaste. "The connection I *do* have with it has to do with the sound that comes out of it." She then goes technical on me, her excursus compensating for my ignorance:

"Because of the nature of the wood that was used to build it, the bridge, the grain, the idiosyncrasies of craftsmanship, right down to the glue that holds it together, it produces a unique voice, an alto voice. It is a voice I found myself specifically drawn to, which makes it a Kmart special that happens to also sound beautiful."

Therein lies the hook, I think. It is in the beauty of the *sound* that she finds value, that sound being a product of connectivity and covenant between instrument and musician. If this violin is of inestimable value to this inestimably talented artist, it is because, unlike any other instrument, it leads her in the direction of the sound she is searching for.

As we speak some more, it becomes clear to me that there is something Regina is *looking* to produce, by which I mean this is unfinished business. She speaks as a woman on a hunt, following the bread crumbs to a destination not yet in sight but glorious in its possibility. Like clay to a potter, the sound that is offered by the instrument is the right but raw material; it must be shaped into something beautiful by the artist, and for her the shaping continues. In many ways music is her life, but it is also in many ways her evolution, a work in progress, a quest. And for this particular woman, it is a quest that began when she was two years old.

## A (WANNABE) STAR IS BORN

Since toddlerhood, Regina has felt a magnetic, genetic attraction to music. As if to imply that it is in her blood, she begins her story by telling me: "My grandmother graduated from Morris Brown College in 1915 with a degree in music, so both music and education were very important in our household. One day when one of my brothers was having his piano lesson at home, my mother told me I walked up to the piano and starting playing the piece he had been practicing. Everyone was shocked because I was only two years old, and no one had shown me how to play. The piano teacher tested me and found I had a gift to hear and play back whatever I heard. This teacher suggested that my mother enroll me in piano lessons." Not long afterward, she started taking lessons on the instrument that, it turns out, was not her heartthrob. "I preferred playing songs I had composed instead of my lessons. My teacher, Anna Love, thought that forcing me to practice and play my lessons would quash my joy for music, so her suggestion was to let me continue playing and composing at home." It was shortly thereafter that this native of Motown was enrolled by her mother in the Detroit Community Music School, where exuberance joined forces with discipline.

"I was taught violin by the Suzuki method," she begins. "Much like learning a language, I was immersed in it." (Indeed, called the "mother tongue" approach by its founder, Shinichi Suzuki, this somewhat controversial method models itself after language learning by stressing early introduction, rote learning, repetition, and effusive encouragement, while minimizing such classical disciplines as the ability to interpret music theory or read musical scores.) Precocious from an early age, Regina displayed a skill for making music that, alas, was not yet matched by an ability to make it *meaningful*. The sound was coming, the significance was not. The clay was taking shape, but still lumpy. In her own words:

"I wanted two things early on," she tells me with the unvarnished frankness I have come to expect from her. "I wanted to be rich, and I wanted to be famous. I wanted to be a star, whatever that meant. And I wanted a star's paycheck, whatever that was." What's more, "I wanted a 'magic violin,' either a Stradivarius or a Guarneri, that would make me into a star." Without asking, I surmise it was the $3 million price tag that would attach to an instrument of either pedigree, combined with the fact that such cash was not exactly lying under the sofa cushions in the Carter household of her youth, that impelled Regina to reconcile her dream with the realization that if fame was going to come at all, it would be with more talent and less instrument. Her situation reminded me of Kipling's directive to "dream, but not make dreams your end."

Fortunately what she did have as an augment to her skills was a wealth of perseverance. Where so many kids with similar dreams let them wither and wane until the slightest distraction blows them asunder, Regina not only stayed with the instrument, she also branched out. By the time she was in high school, when other kids' starter guitars, double-bladed ice skates, and ballet slippers were sitting in the back of the closet, gathering dust, she was not only fluent in violin but conversant in viola, oboe, and voice as well, and performing with the Detroit Symphony Youth Orchestra (later named the Detroit Civic Orchestra). She still wanted to be a star, but she was also coming to love the sound for the sound's sake.

It was while in high school that the steady diet of classical music she had been getting fed was ever so slightly spiced when friend and fellow musician Carla Cook (who would go on to a very gratifying jazz career of her own) gave Regina a taste of the likes of jazz giants Ella Fitzgerald, Stéphane Grappelli, Noel Pointer, and Eddie Jefferson. "That was my first introduction to jazz," she notes, her hands swiping the air as if simulating an explosion, "and I was totally blown away."

Having been trained all those years in the rigors of European music, Regina reacted to jazz's free-floating anarchy the way a caged bird might react to an open gate and an absent keeper. "Man, you can *do* this?!" she asked Carla, incredulously. It was as though jazz musicians were the subversive gang in the neighborhood, musical graffitists in the business of violating some sacred creed for which they would be summarily punished by the guardians of the classical flame.

Perhaps it was because she was more intimidated than enticed, or perhaps it was because she continued to hone and refine that elusive sound, but whatever the reason, Regina set out to continue her classical studies at the New England Conservatory. Her mother wanted her to have a steady job with an orchestra or teaching so she would have benefits and social security. She didn't think jazz musicians made any money and was disturbed by the lifestyle. But in due course the siren's song got the better of Regina: she decided to switch her concentration to jazz, discovered that the conservatory offered no such discipline specifically for violin, and transferred to Oakland University to study with saxophonist Doc Martin Holladay and the renowned trumpeter Marcus Belgrave. (Belgrave rose to prominence in the 1950s as Ray Charles's lead horn and in 2008 was bestowed the much deserved honorific "Jazz Master Laureate of Detroit.")

Her tenure at Oakland and the years immediately following represented the formative era in her career, punctuated by stints with big bands, a couple of CD recordings with a combo called The String Trio of New York, and gigs in which she accompanied the likes of Aretha Franklin, Billy Joel, and Max Roach. By 1995, when she released her first solo album, the eponymous *Regina Carter*, she was on her way. The sound, while still a thing in formation, had nestled into its idiomatic home. It was jazz.

## IT'S NOT SO SIMPLE

But with success came complexity: the more she honed her sound, the more she developed a fan base. And the more she developed a fan base, the more fans came to expect of her. She wasn't just making music; she was also making a living, and art and commerce are not always easy bedfellows. Two interlocking stories tell of the price Regina paid for her growth as a jazz musician.

"I was contracted to play a festival in another country (we can't say where, *please*)," she begins, "but I was told my mom, who had been battling cancer for the fourth time, was dying. The long and the short of it is that I canceled the gig to be with her, and the next thing I know, I'm being sued for the cancellation." She was infuriated by the lawsuit, devastated by the death of her mother, and disenchanted by the realization that almighty lucre could be a corrupting influence in the making of music.

"The lawsuit lasted over a year, and they came at me personally. I was angry, really, really angry," she says, and then adds, with great insight, "What I remember most was being angry at music, at being a musician, and this really surprised me."

It may have surprised her, but it made sense, really, because up to this point music had been a pure thing for her. Now, with her evolution as an artist, she was butting heads with the impurities that attach to the art when there is money to be made—or lost—by it. She also came to see a rough parallel between the lawsuit and her mother's death because it's not an exaggeration to say that in both instances something of profound intimacy was summarily taken away from her. She acted out the only way she knew how, and this is the second of the interlocking stories.

"This all hit me at such a raw and vulnerable place. Then, without even realizing it, it all came out in my music. I started playing with rage, real rage. And if the audience didn't feel my rage, as it often didn't, I got even angrier."

What's worse, "when my mom died the darkness of what I was feeling came through in my music, but people didn't understand that tunes I once played with some lightness might come out heavy, sad, because that's what I was feeling. I resented people's questioning me, and I resented that I was being made to feel as though I had to get up on stage and put on an act, put on a show. Managers wanted it 'corrected.' Businesspeople wanted me to entertain." She pauses, thoughtfully. Her hands are clasped between her knees, and her head is down, contemplative. "And look, I get that, I get that people want to be entertained," she adds, generously, her voice ever so beseeching. "But I can only be honest. If I'm gonna do this [performing], then I will have to be honest. I won't smile when I'm sad." No minstrel, she.

That was a big "if," because like a lover who was less spurned than cuckolded, Regina wanted out. Brutalized by the money people, misunderstood by her fan base, and aggrieved at the death of her mother, she had had enough of searching for the sound. Or so she thought.

## REGINA CARTER 2.0

When Regina owned up to her desire to quit, she acknowledged that "there was still that part of me that wanted to be a star, the part that said, 'What in the world are you talkin' about!?'" This helped her to see her sentiments as less enduring than the consequences of capitulating to them. Instead of either bailing out or forging on, she struck a middle ground. "I backed off working so hard, eased up on my schedule." Partially in response to the care she showed her mother in her dying days, Regina also wandered into some new territory.

"I began to get more interested in the science of music, and how music can help people heal. I took an interest in music therapy, but when I did so, I came to see that that wasn't finally what I was looking for because I was looking for the magic in music to control emotions rather than the music unleashing emotions, as it did for me when I got so enraged. I'm still looking."

Unbeknownst to her, in 2006 her search would be given a significant boost.

## THE GIFT OF GENIUS

In live performances with jazz veterans and in ensembles, [Regina Carter] captivates her audience with the passion and spirit of adventure intrinsic to her approach to music. Through artistry with an instrument that has been defined predominantly by the classical tradition, Carter is pioneering new possibilities for the violin and for jazz.

These were just some of the encomiums used by the John D. and Catherine T. MacArthur Foundation to describe one of their 2006 Genius Grant recipients. The prestigious $500,000 fellowships are awarded annually to a select number of "talented individuals who have shown extraordinary originality and dedication in their creative pursuits and a marked capacity for self-direction." For Regina, it was not only validation; it was also liberation because the money allowed her to exercise her "capacity for self-direction" in a way that would mark yet another turning point in the evolution of her music, the search for her sound.

In relating it, Regina recalls what she has already told me about the need to be authentic not only in the music she composes but also in the way she chooses to perform it. Describing her maturation as an artist, she tells me, "I believe I'm more honest now. And the MacArthur helped me get there. It gave me the space to do my work the way I wanted, without an eye toward whether or not people will like it."

The "work" she is talking about is *Reverse Thread*, an elegant paean to the folk traditions prevalent in the music of so many cultures, but traditions that trace their birth and nourishment to the African continent. It is a work she has thought about for some time, and MacArthur made it possible. And as it happens, the people *do* like it. She explains its origins and its meaning:

"Having grown up in Detroit, I was exposed to so many different cultures," she explains, as together we tick off some of the cultural exposures—Senegalese, Ugandan, Egyptian, Cajun, Greek, Jordanian, Chaldean, Irish—we both recall from having lived there. "With this project I began by considering not only where I am now but also where I came from musically. Like pulling a thread on a cloth, you zigzag back, reverse the thread, until you find the cloth's origin. My musical origins were tied up in all of this diverse music I came upon while growing up in Detroit."

With this as her backdrop, she was heavily influenced by what she detected in much of this music to be a scale system that wasn't traditionally Western, one that made room for a whole host of exotic stringed instruments. Regina wanted to make what she called a "world music record" in which her violin—still regarded by some purists as an interloper in the horn-, bass-, and keyboard-heavy world of jazz—could feel right at home with all the other strings.

"I began by looking into music from the many different cultures of Africa," much of which has found its way into the

album. The gentle "Hiwumbe Awumba" is based on recordings from Ugandan Jews, the festive "Zerapiki" was inspired
by accordion-based music from Madagascar, and the source
waters for "Daydreaming on the Niger" are self-explanatory.
But while so much of the music is rooted in Africa, it would
be limiting to brand *Reverse Thread* Afrocentric since the hin-
terlands of both Europe and the Americas prevail as well, if
more subtly, with vestiges of jigs, polkas, and Cajun rhythms
seeping into a number of cuts. The end result is not only a
global experience; it is also an experience that tends much
more toward the universal language of the folk tradition (a
tradition, as any denizen of the Mississippi bayou can attest,
never far from the jazz argot) than anything Regina has hith-
erto taken on.

"It wasn't an easy birth," she confesses. "It took over two
years to produce," often with "changes coming to me literally in my sleep. In my *sleep!*" Perhaps the hardest part of the
process, she recalls, was "letting go, and letting it be what it
wanted to be. I can only dictate what I want it to be, what I
think it is supposed to be. I provide the ingredients, but the
instruments have a certain amount of leeway." (In addition
to Carter on violin, the album includes two accordions, two
basses, one percussion, and a West African 21-stringed bridge
harp known as a kora.) Her spin on this, her "letting go,"
reminds me of the title of the old Barry Stevens meditation:
"Don't Push the River (It Flows by Itself)."

"With all of the difficulty," I asked, "did you give birth to
the child you wanted to give birth to?" Evidently she did.

"It actually exceeded my expectations," Regina answered.
As she tells me this it is clear, based on what she had said
about the intent of the project, that she does not measure her
success in terms of broad audience appeal (though it has been
forthcoming) but on her ability to take an idea whose origins
lie in the city of her origin, and translate that idea into a sound.

In fact, it takes some work to listen to *Reverse Thread*. As Regina put it, "I wanted to draw people in. It's very quiet, subtle." More Brubeck than Bird, "it requires attentive listening. People are forced to listen" if they are going to fully appreciate the amalgam of music, the weaving of so many different threads that Regina is presenting them with.

So the search for the sound is grounded in the need to listen, something Regina Carter can request of her audience because it is something she has spent a lifetime demanding of herself. Perhaps as the granddaughter of a music major from "Morris Brown College, class of 1915," one could say she was born with a compulsion to search that sound; it was in her blood. From here it took her to the piano, which wasn't quite right, then on to violin, which was. Classical training brought a refinement of skills but a dissatisfaction for what she felt was a cosseted style not entirely to her liking. Jazz was to her liking, however, and with the discovery of her affinity to the idiom, she was off and running. But even jazz presented obstacles when the purity of the sound was vitiated by the demands of an industry in which artistic expression often runs at cross-purposes with financial success. Jazz is, as the artist herself put it, a hard life. When the MacArthurs made life a little less hard, she not only listened more, but also more intently and with more freedom, as the sound carried her to four continents, delivering to her the raw material of music that is as old as humanity itself, but put into her hands, has become a new thing.

By her own definition, she is "not there yet" and may never be. The search may be lifelong, echoing the old Tolkien adage that "not all those who wander are lost." Like a parlor game where each clue points the player to the next one, Regina will continue to refine her calling, perhaps now with a twist:

Her earlier dalliance with the idea of becoming a music therapist was brief, but as a result of her mother's illness, something profound happened that has not only left an indelible mark on her; it has also, quite possibly, pointed her to the next clue.

"When my mother was making her transition," she muses, "she couldn't communicate anymore. But . . ."—Regina pauses, smiles a reflective smile, as a poignant moment from long ago is being relived as if in the present tense—"she could still hear. Could still listen." There it is again, I think to myself: the fathomless gift of listening.

"So sometimes I would take my music in, and I would play for her. And I would see her responding. Her vital signs would tell me that she was hearing me. That's when I realized, 'Oh, there's really something to this.'" She speaks a little more expansively now:

"There was a lot of history between my mom and me, a lot of emotion." This is clearly not easy territory for her to traverse, but it is not my business to ask of the roots of that emotion or the content of that history. It is also beside the point. So I keep quiet and hope that my silence will encourage her to continue with her thoughts.

"In the end, though, it was a gift for me to be able to be there and take care of her as I did. I gave myself over to being her caretaker, and I did it with love. And with music. And with bed making and medicating and feeding, the whole bit." A mother-daughter relationship, complicated (as so many are) but not abnormally so, became clarified, a matter of unmitigated grace.

As we sit in brief silence I tell her of a line from a song by the New Orleans group, The Subdudes, that seems appropriate to what she is saying. From their single, a boozy, bluesy ballad called "Made of Stone," I play the refrain for her:

Carry on, and have yourself a lovely ride.
Think of me, when you finally reach the other side.

"Yeah," she tells me, "that's pretty much it."

I ask her, "So as a musician, what do you take away from the experience of your mother's passing?"

"I want to make music that is therapeutic. I want to play music that means something to you [the listener], something that you love."

As she extrapolates from her experience with her mother's last days and tries to identify the broader lesson for her as a musician and as a human being, I sense that a piece of her unfinished business has to do with her relationship to those who listen to her. Early on in her formation she wanted to be famous, wanted fans to know and adore her. But as fame descended upon her, she discovered that with adoration comes expectation, which in turn impinges upon freedom. It doesn't free the artist: quite the contrary, it chokes her, distracts her from the quest for her sound. From here, though, with the creation of *Reverse Thread* she has reclaimed her freedom, made music for music's sake, and as serendipity would desire, it has an audience.

Now, when she thinks of all the stops thus far along the trail, and incorporates both her mother's illness and her own healing presence in the face of that illness, she seems to realize that in pursuit of her sound, she does not want to leave the "other" out of the equation. Instead, in some approximate way she wants to do for the listener what she did for her mother. That is, she wants to give to that person the kind of sound that is a tonic for what ails them, that they can love, and that eases whatever "transition" large or small might be their lot at the moment it wafts from her magical hands to their grateful ears.

## POSTSCRIPTS

The little girl wanted to be rich and famous, with those riches and that fame delivered to her by dint of a "magic violin" of the Stradivarian ilk. Instead, a woman, now grown into middle age, plays a Kmart special and lives the hard life that is the lot of virtually all jazz musicians who are serious enough about their craft not to make compromises at the altar of expediency.

Still, if she has not realized that childish dream, perhaps by outgrowing it, she has inadvertently approximated it. As for fame, she has toured internationally, played with the likes of Lyman Woodard, Marcus Belgrave, and Ray Brown, and been cited for her "nimble prowess" by *New York Times* jazz critic Nate Chinen. In the small but burgeoning world of jazz strings, she is a vanguard.

As for fortune, I remind her of the old joke, "How do you amass a small fortune as a jazz musician? You start out with a large one." "Ain't that the truth!" she tells me. The fact is, she has made a living, and a life, in one of the most unforgiving artistic mediums imaginable. And more important, she has not sold her soul to do it.

As for the Kmart special that will have to suffice as her magic wand, there was in fact a time some years ago when she got a taste of something just a little more high end and somewhat magical. In December of 2001, in a show of solidarity after the attacks of 9/11, the Italian city of Genoa invited Regina to perform a concert using a priceless 260-year-old handcrafted violin that had been the property of Niccolò Paganini. Nicknamed *Il Cannone*, "The Cannon," for its enormous sound, and jealously guarded in a Genovese vault, Carter was one of the few musicians—and the first jazz musician—ever so honored. The concert was such a success that she was then invited back to record an album with the venerable instrument. Thus was born *Paganini: After a Dream*, a classical/jazz fusion about which the critic Dan McClenaghan wrote in *All about Jazz*: "From the very opening notes, it is obvious that Paganini's violin is an extraordinary instrument in the gentle hands of a passionate lover."

The only problem, as Carter acknowledges, was that after she had played the majestic cannon and her own instrument was returned to her, "I went to play it, and it sounded like a mouse. So small a sound."

But it is that sound, however small and however humbly rooted in her own instrument, that is her true love and her singular pursuit. In truth, the thing she values most she may never have, never fully attain. She will always be on that treasure hunt, always finding something that leads her to a place whence she can make that sound richer or gentler or in some other way more to her liking both as a musician who needs to produce the sound and as a human being who needs to deliver it to others. She is a long-distance runner for whom there is no finish line. As she puts it:

"There are times when I am on stage performing [with my band] when it is just transcendent. Everyone is having it, everyone knows that we've just falling into it, an arabesque. That is when I am in alignment with God, when I feel that I am with God. Spiritual, clean, not doctrinaire. Not something I have to discuss or fight someone over. There are times when the ecstatic happens. Times, every once in a while, when we experience the bliss. And those moments? They are a gift."

∞

Regina's story reminds me of the observation my old friend Tim Smith, Riverside Church's former Music Director, made when he said, "I find the term 'sacred music' to be redundant to the point of utter irrelevancy." Tim was getting at the fact that all music has the capacity to transport us to deeper, richer, other places, and in this way music is sacred insofar as it is performing a sacred task. I feel the same way about sacred space: any space is as sacred as the activities we engage in when we occupy that space.

That said, the reverse can be true as well. Music intended to be sacred—hymns, masses, cantatas—can fail in its attempt to serve God and mammon, and when it does, it might not be the fault of the composer.

To the first point, we have only to listen to the dark, cool, soothing rhythm of John Coltrane's "A Love Supreme" to be caught up in the feeling that we are floating, enwombed and weightless, in a sea of serenity. Blithe, blissful, but not giddy, Coltrane's composition calls to mind some words of the Deuteronomist: "The eternal God is your dwelling place, and underneath are the everlasting arms" (Deut. 33:26). It is in those everlasting arms that we float, in exuberant reverence for a cradling God come to us in the guise of a tenor sax.

At another extreme, haunting but no less holy, consider Bob Dylan's "A Hard Rain's Gonna Fall," with its edgy, apocalyptic images of crooked highways and sad forests, the roar of a wave that could drown the world, the one person starving and many people laughing, and of course, "the song of the poet who died in the gutter." Told from the perspective of the young son who cannot help but "reflect from the mountain" in the hopes that all souls will hear his witness, it is a hymn of accountability and a Cassandra call. No more prophetic piece of music came out of the 1960s' rock scene than this.

For that matter, Regina Carter's irenic interpretation of the Mali guitarist Habib Koité's composition "N'Teri" has a transcendent, hypnotic quality suggestive of Koité's lyrics (conveyed but not sung on Carter's version): "You met me with a smile / God will return it to you." To hear her rendition is to feel the smile and believe in the beneficence of a God who has already returned it.

On the other hand, who among us has not been brought low by a less than worshipful worship service, the one in the stuffy, weary, half-empty church, long ago sucked dry of any vestige of enthusiasm it once enjoyed, in which a narcoleptic congregation groans its way, off-key, through a larghetto version of "Joyful, Joyful, We Adore Thee"? You feel about as much joy as a daylily in a summer drought. There is no adoration, no *joie* as you silently count the beats until the last note is struck and Beethoven stops spinning in his grave.

Sound is made sacred, and noise is made joyful by a confluence of two circumstances: the artist offers it expression, and the recipient accords it respect. This is why Regina finds such worth in *Reverse Thread*, and she will continue to find worth in future endeavors. It is because the musicians do their part, but the audience must do theirs as well. Not unlike prayer itself, the sacred sound is not monologue: it is conversation.

## Questions for Discussion

1. How can sound serve to stir our emotions and direct our actions, either for good or for ill? Give examples. Can silence have the same power?

2. Carter says of a particularly grim time in her life, "When my mom died, the darkness of what I was feeling came through in my music, but people didn't understand that tunes I once played with some lightness might come out heavy, sad, because that's what I was feeling. I resented people's questioning me, and I resented that I was being made to feel as though I had to get up on stage and put on an act, put on a show." What is the artist's responsibility to her audience especially when it conflicts with her responsibility to herself? What is the lesson to be gleaned for those of us who are not artists or who do not have audiences?

3. The MacArthur grant provided Carter with opportunities that would not otherwise have been available to her. There are those who misquote Scripture when they

say, "Money is the root of all evil." The accurate quote, from 1 Timothy 6:10 is, "*The love of* money is the root of all evil" (KJV). Discuss how money holds no inherent moral valence but can assume moral dimensions depending upon how it is "loved" or hated, used or avoided.

# Chapter 7

# CHRISTOPHER LIM
## *The Wise Young Man*

*What one knows is, in youth, of little moment;*
*they know enough to know how to learn.*
—Henry Adams

WHEN CHRISTOPHER LIM WAS FOURTEEN YEARS OLD AND A FRESH-
man in high school, a classmate, a young girl, was struck by a
car and suffered what were diagnosed as life-threatening injuries. As one might expect, the incident rattled the girl's friends,
most of whom had lived their lives largely insulated from tragedy of this magnitude. But as the child slowly mended, her
classmates found their bearings again, rallying to support her
in ways you might expect from young adolescents. They visited, joked, gossiped, told stories. Some brought her stuffed
animals, others candy bars, others homework, others balloons.
Lots of balloons.

Chris visited too, but instead of balloons, he brought a
musical composition he wrote in the girl's honor, a deceptively intricate duet for piano and violin in E-flat major that
he and another classmate performed and recorded. It was
suffused with a soothing melody and intended, in his words,
"to offer serenity in the face of upheaval and release in the

face of tension." Listening to it is to be adrift in a kind of acoustic shiatsu. It did not sound like the work of a fourteen-year-old, either in complexity of arrangement or fluidity of execution.

This was seven years ago, and the intervening years have seen no atrophy in this prodigy's creative muscles. In the remaining years of his high school career, Chris spent off-hours studying music at Julliard's precollege program, performing at such esteemed venues as Lincoln Center, Tanglewood, and Boston's Jordan Hall. In 2010, after having been elected to Phi Beta Kappa as a college junior, Chris graduated summa cum laude from Harvard with joint degrees in music and mathematics. Though discretionary time was at a premium in those years, he nevertheless managed to devote a sizeable chunk of it to performing music for shut-ins in Boston-area hospitals and senior centers.

Slight of build and youthful in appearance, I can imagine people not only continuing to call Chris a prodigy well into his thirties but also asking him for proof of age should he sidle up to a bar. A first-generation Korean-American, his creaseless features are what Westerners might call fine, almost delicate. His hair is dark, wispy, cut neat, and kept short. He is well groomed and handsome in an understated way. As if to belie his powerhouse résumé, he bears his accomplishments with a modesty bordering on self-effacement. Words like "awards" and "distinctions," when referring to his own, come out of his mouth only with reluctance and much prodding. When by necessity he refers to something laudable he has done, he tends to look away from me, as though we have broached an unseemly subject. His normally relaxed mien gives way to an eagerness to move on.

What pulls him out of his reticent fugue is the opportunity to share with me what it is he would pull out of his fire. "It is the ability to learn." he tells me, voice quickening, eyes brightening, once-clasped hands now raised and in full wave, as though he is conducting the last rousing bars of a Vivaldi concerto (or perhaps a Lim sonata). "If I had to isolate what I would keep in the face of losing everything else, it would be the ability to learn or to change," he says. "I see these two things as very much related if not the same."

When I suggest that it is possible to change without learning (making new mistakes rather than old ones) but not vice versa, he both concedes the point and then refines it by declaring that learning, for him, entails coming "to see something through someone else's point of view, their opinions and experiences, their core beliefs, all of which invite me to change."

As our conversation begins to track this thought in a little greater detail, I am given to believe that Chris is drawn to learning for what it offers to add to his life and to change for what it offers to subtract from it.

"When I listen to someone else's point of view" about something, "I am open to learning from what I hear, but this entails some risk. The risk, of course, is that beliefs I once held might have to be altered or even abandoned," he says. Since most people in their early twenties, especially those who hover in the rarefied strata of the intellectually and academically elite, are more eager to brandish their knowledge than to subject it to public scrutiny, Chris's keenness to use learning as a means to bring his own beliefs into question strikes me as characteristic of someone astute beyond his years. No wonder Chris then venerates learning so; he has benefited more than expected at an age when intelligence is halfway to the stars while wisdom is still sitting on the launchpad.

As he speaks more about the dynamics of learning, it becomes clear that there are two rudiments to his equation: Learning as gathering, and learning as adjusting. Put another way, in the world according to Chris, in order to learn, you must be able to do these two things: remember and forget.

## AUS NICHTS

*Aus nichts* (Heb. 11:3, *Luther Bibel*). "From nothing." This old German term, referring to God's creation of the heavens and the earth, seems a fitting way to describe one element in the creation of Chris's universe of knowledge. As he describes the process, it becomes clear that gathering wisdom is for him the easiest and, not surprisingly, the least interesting. "One way to think of learning is to imagine going through doors where, on the other side, are things I know nothing about," he tells me, and then relates it to his schooling: "Classroom learning is like this. In fact, a part of my college education can be thought of in this way. You take courses in subjects you've never explored. You meet new people, live in a new city, experience new living arrangements, try new foods." Shifting metaphors, he adds, "It's a little like having a basket with empty space in it into which you are putting new things." What he is talking about is perhaps the most elemental method of learning, the method we first begin to master as young children, when our ability to absorb is more sophisticated than our ability to interpret. Perhaps it is because of its apparent lack of subtlety that Chris skates over it so lightly, eager to move on to the kind of learning that most intrigues him.

## A LOSER'S GAME

"One of the hardest things to come to terms with is that in order to learn we need not only to gather in but also to toss out." Chris tosses out this little Zen-like zinger and lets it hang in midair like a misted, mystifying aroma we are meant to draw in and contemplate, before then explaining himself.

"If all we have is the stuff we've put in the basket, then we risk hanging on to old ideas even when we may have outgrown them. I think we have to let our beliefs be challenged.

We need to question them, and when those questions don't have adequate answers, sometimes we have to abandon them. Sometimes we have to take things *out of* the basket."

When he says this, I hear the faint refrain of what the religious call a willingness to experience a conversion of heart: "I once was lost, but now am found," wrote the hymnist John Newton (in "Amazing Grace!"), and as the psalmist put it, "Incline my heart to your testimonies" (Ps. 119:36 ESV). The apostle Paul stated it this way: "When I was a child, I spoke like a child" (1 Cor. 13:11). In such instances, Chris explains to me, we have to be ready to take a good hard look at what we *think* we know to be true. But more than this, we have to be willing to grow beyond these sometimes childish beliefs and youthful inclinations, to be willing to surrender them, however dearly we hold them and however well they've served us, when they fail to withstand the rigors of that examination. Then he offers an example that strikes particularly close to home for him, because it is about music.

Having played the piano since he was seven, Chris has come to see music not simply as something he does but as fundamental to his self-definition. It is, in his words, "very much a part of how I think, my daily life, like a part of my body, not extrinsic to me." For Chris, music is more ontological than functional; it is an "I am" statement, a statement of who he is rather than simply one of many things he does and does well. It was with this baggage that he set off in the summer of 2010, a newly minted college grad, for an advanced music program at which he would receive world-class training in piano composition.

What he didn't know was that early in his stay, he would run headlong into the one instructor who not only set her bar high; she also had little patience for anyone who failed to reach it. As he tells it:

"I went to the program and I played for her. Very demanding. I have never performed for anyone as . . . ," he pauses, searching, as it were, for just the right note to strike a balance between diplomacy and accuracy in describing her. "Um, I've never played for anyone as *severe* as she.

"I had seen her teach, so I knew what it would be like to be in her crosshairs. Nonetheless after my first time of playing for her, I felt as though I had lost everything. When I was done playing, she simply said, dismissively, 'There's nothing there.'"

Fourteen years of study, countless accolades, hours and ovations, academic distinctions, and acceptance into the prestigious New England Conservatory for the following fall—all, in this instructor's harsh assessment, chimera. Smoke and mirrors. Not talent, just the illusion of talent. Her assessment of Chris's work devastated him.

"I'd certainly had individual sessions with teachers who would be tough on me," Chris recalled, "but no instructor had ever left me feeling as though I had absolutely nothing. This woman, for whom I eventually played several times, left me feeling empty." Nothing in the basket!

But this is where his abiding reverence for learning kicks in. "In retrospect," he tells me, he came to see her genius. "Though it was spirit-crushing, it was also in a way refreshing to shelve any skills I'd acquired to this point and start from scratch. In order to learn from her, I had to adapt, which meant putting aside all that I'd learned before coming to the program. It was still anxiety producing to work with her, but now" he came to understand it not just as gratuitous malevolence but "as tyranny for the sake of growth." Chris's analysis reminded me of the old adage popular in competitive athletics: when the coach *stops* screaming at you, you're in trouble, because it means you're no longer worth his effort. If rejection is the penultimate putdown, the ultimate is indifference.

Chris then expanded his thinking on the matter, observing that while he chose to adapt to the situation by, at least tacitly, giving credence to Lady Voldemort's assessment of his work, he did have other options. "I could have responded with denial, anger, resistance, or defensiveness, but they wouldn't have put me in a position to learn from this instructor," he points out. Put another way, he could've led with his ego. In a larger sense he is telling me that there are occasions when learning (of any kind) requires putting that ego in cold storage, emptying oneself of old assumptions, old knowledge, or old skills (even those skills that have been highly rewarded in the past) in order to make room for something new.

There is an implicit humility that applies more broadly to Chris's kind of learning, a willingness to confess that there are times when once serviceable ideas no longer hold up for us ("When I was a child, . . . I thought like a child" [1 Cor. 13:11]), and I ask Chris if he saw such humility as common currency among people of his age and station. When I put the question to him, I was thinking in particular of his years at Harvard, a school that is, at least by all American standards, the mother of all prestigious academic institutions. (Crimson alums are rightly proud, for instance, of being graduates of the oldest university in North America if only the 72nd oldest in the world.) "Humility" is not a word frequently associated with the Crimson lexicon. If anything, the opposite is true; Harvardians brandish their accomplishments with the same high-beam directness that Chris Lim downplays his. And if humility did not come easily to students at a place like Harvard, wouldn't that prove an impediment to their learning?

By now, because I am getting used to the verbal dexterity he so deftly exercises in his choice of words, I am not surprised when he finesses my question. "In general, I would say that students at all levels at an elite institution come in with a sense of success," he begins. "And I think it's natural to want to hang on to that success. You feel like you've earned it. You don't want to let it go." By his own admission, he is reflecting on both his mind-set and that of his erstwhile colleagues, but then he shifts to a completely self-referential perspective, adding: "I enjoyed my first year of college, but it was only over time that I became a better student. Over time my work ethic grew and was honed. I learned how to learn." Expanding on this, he goes on to explain how Harvard, with a thick hide of erudition, may not be the easiest place in the world for a student to admit to the vast sea of knowledge that *isn't* in his command; but with a little maturing, a guy like him can at least come to admit it to himself. And when he does, he becomes a more learned learner.

Although by all indications he is congenitally brilliant, disciplined, and industrious, it is ultimately this modesty that makes Chris such an avid and able (let alone likeable) learner, and why, by extension, he values learning so highly. What's more encouraging, he seems to have an intuitive understanding of the fact that modesty is more than an admirable trait: it is a self-sustaining pedagogical asset. As long as he comes at new adventures with humility, he will learn from them. By extension, as long as he learns from them, he will find his humility rewarded and therefore reinforced. While raw knowledge risks arrogance, earned wisdom begets modesty. As they might say within the ivied walls of Cambridge, *quod erat demonstrandum*, "what was demonstrated."

## EXTRACURRICULAR EDUCATION

As we bat around this notion of what we come to refer to as "utile humility," Chris shifts his college recollections from academic achievement to personal growth and how the same constraint, the same need to be willing to empty oneself, applies to young people like himself who, while intellectually precocious can also be developmentally pedestrian.

"Over time," he begins, "I became bothered by a certain self-consciousness that I saw in myself and in a lot of my classmates. We were very obsessed with our image. It wasn't a question of 'Who am I?' so much as it was 'How do I want others to see [perceive] me?' And it wasn't just physical image; it was also all aspects of our identity." With this question he is now pushing himself out of the classroom and into the larger educational arena that is the university environment as a whole, that halfway house between childhood and adulthood, and wondering if this identity polishing is one of the perils that young people attending a high-caliber school might be particularly prone to.

"We want identities that show us off, probably because we stood out in high school. We were successful enough to get into a good college, but then we arrive and we're surrounded with people who were just as successful, so we look for new ways to distinguish ourselves. We look for identities that [we think] will exude success." Chris gets to the nub of the issue when he observes of his undergraduate self and his classmates, "We have a need for the approval of others, of our peers. We look for validation. We look to fit into a niche in the social environment, and so we tailor an image to conform to the rules of the niche that we choose for ourselves." A tribe of geniuses, alas, is still a tribe.

As he looks back on this experience, he now sees it as not only burdensome but also counterproductive. "This [image obsession] stifles learning because it turns me in on myself. I become self-absorbed. I am deprived of seeing anything other than what I want to project. In the interest of wanting others to see me in a certain light, I lose humility." Then he adds, almost as an afterthought, "It's also tiring."

"Do you know where you really see this played out?" he asks me, before answering his own question. "On Facebook." Facebook! The coin of the social media realm, born and incubated just a few years earlier at—where else?—Harvard. Chris explains:

"The whole Facebook zeitgeist is very much about self-expression, but we use it to express images of ourselves that we think will make positive impressions on others." Solicitous of my ignorance about the medium, he then goes on to explain to me how people, such as himself, would tailor what they would post—writings, photographs, intellectual banter, and the like—on their Facebook wall with an eye toward making a good impression on others who would visit the site. "I don't think it's a conscious activity," he allows, "but I do think that on some subliminal level we're [choosing particular artifacts to post] so that other people will see them and think well of us." He then loops back to his veneration of learning: "If learning is the pursuit of some sort of truth, this countermands it because it stresses artifice."

The desire to be well thought of by others is by all measures a common human impulse (think of how often, when meeting new people, we "lead with our résumé" rather than, say, our trove of "life's most embarrassing moments," a list that for most of us is both longer and far more amusing). But it is even more prevalent among adolescents, who, as they begin to psychically and physically separate from their family of origin, experience a need for peer identification that is felt most acutely in these teen and early postteen years. Chris seemed to be not only instinctively aware of this, but aware as well of how an achievement- and prestige-driven environment such as the campus of a major university would only serve to up the ante to toxic proportions. He also put both this instinct and his native modesty to good use in deciding that he was as prone to this approval seeking as anyone else, and that it only impeded his true love, his love of learning.

As we begin to wind down our initial conversation, I make a mental note that Chris has just finished the first half of a two-year graduate program in music composition at the New

England Conservatory, and I ask him if professional considerations are beginning to take shape for when he finishes the degree.

"Oh, I'm not pursuing music professionally," he tells me, dismissively. "When I'm done with the program, I'll be applying to medical school."

I guess I shouldn't be surprised that this young man who sees music as a part of his very being is not interested in seeing it as a paycheck, nor should I be surprised that the discipline he has chosen to pursue is not only exacting but also something he barely prepared himself for in college. Instead of treating Harvard as a kind of high-caliber voc-tech school, a place of preparation for a lifetime of labor, he saw it as a place to pursue his passion for the sake of passion itself. And to learn how to learn. There is a purity to his approach, and I can't help but admire a young man who values that purity even at the price of making the path toward his chosen profession—a long and arduous task to begin with—even longer and more arduous to navigate. When he heads off to medical school, his basket will be much less flush than those of his premed counterparts. He will have work to do.

When I ask Chris if he has considered what branch of medicine he would like to pursue, he responds with an answer that seems perfectly suited to his character. "I am interested in palliative care," he informs me. "I would like to help people relieve their suffering as they prepare to die." He embellishes his thoughts a little with reflections on his own life and beliefs: "I did some study of Buddhism when I was in school, and one of the things that made a great deal of sense to me was the Buddhist understanding of the impermanence of all things and, by extension, the need to know how to 'let go.'

"Western medicine doesn't do much to acknowledge death," he continues, "but it should. Death is not a failure, as some doctors see it; it is a mystery and an inevitability. It is also meaningful: without the reality of death, we would not value life the way most of us do. It [life] would not have the same meaning. Death is there to be embraced."

From here, he and I return to the broader idea of impermanence. Chris points out that to experience impermanence is to experience "little deaths." A relationship ends, or a career comes to a halt. We are forced to move out of town, or a daughter grows into adulthood and leaves home. A young child discovers that there is no Santa Claus, or a young soldier comes to believe that there is no God. In these and countless other instances, we are given a small taste of death, of the ending of something. We grieve and rage, we reflect and adjust. All things we will do again when the door of death itself is near and beginning to creak open to our own arrival. It is Chris's intention to be there for others as that begins to happen.

There are two reasons why I believe Chris is suited to this field of medicine. First, his love of learning is not grounded in any suppressed need to become a master of this or that art form. Quite the opposite, it is grounded in a profound respect for all he *doesn't* know. He is eager not only to take in new ideas but also to have established ideas questioned, scrutinized, rethought, reworked, revised, maybe even abandoned. What better disposition to bring to that greatest of all unknowns, death itself?

And second, his inveterate modesty immunizes Chris from the messiah complex that afflicts those would-be doctors for whom death is synonymous with failure. I believe he will be able to impart healing care even, or perhaps especially, to the dying, and I say this because—just as the word "heal," from the old English *hāl*, means, among other things, "whole"—I believe Chris will have a unique talent for allowing his patients to step through that doorway with a sense of completeness. Under his care they will know not only that death is the natural consequence of life; they will know as well that a compassionate physician who has done all in his power to make their journey comfortable has kept steady company with them. They will know this because in his care they will be learned learners, and he will teach them. When I imagine him years from now being a healing presence to the frightened, the frail, and the uncertain, I can hear the refrain of the old ballad "Brokedown Palace," popularized some years ago by the Grateful Dead:

> Goin' home, goin' home
> By the waterside I will rest my bones . . .

I would be remiss if I don't ask Chris whether there is any point at which he sees music and medicine intersect. In what way does he become, not just a doctor, but also a musician who practices medicine? Ever the thoughtful one, he chews on this for a minute before telling me, "In both disciplines you really have to be aware of who your audience is. You have to consider where they are at that moment, and you have to ask yourself, 'What is it in this experience that I want them to come away with?'"

When he tells me this, I *don't* imagine him years from now. My mind doesn't immediately jump to the young doctor at the bedside of an elderly patient whose slowing pulse Chris is paying close attention to as he holds her worn and weathered hand in his. Instead, I think of him years earlier, at the bedside of a young friend, the sounds of his duet for piano and violin, soft, sweet, and dulcet, offering "serenity in the face of upheaval and release in the face of tension."

It's a wonderful way to learn how to live. And when the time comes, not a bad way to learn how to die.

Once I saw a bumper sticker, affixed to a car owned by a distant acquaintance, declaring a faith that has always underscored for me the fine line that exists between conviction and fanaticism. In big bold letters it proclaimed:

THE BIBLE SAYS IT, I BELIEVE IT,
THAT SETTLES IT!

The sticker's "My way or the highway" screed-like tone was rather representative of this guy's worldview. Long on judgment and short on love, he had an annoying habit of parading opinion as fact but had no patience for countervailing sentiments, regardless of how logical the premise, reasoned the argument, or heartfelt the sentiment. The earth was created 6,000 years ago, Methuselah lived to be 969, corn and wheat grown in the same field at the same time are a Levitical sin, women should be submissive to their husbands, and Christianity is the only game in town.

As an army of one, he was harmless enough; but as one of many (I assume the bumper-sticker company did a brisk business in proselytizing his particular gospel of intolerance), he becomes representative of a movement that threatens to imperil faith in the interest of protecting it. If we cannot open ourselves to the possibility that the ideas of others can broaden our horizons, then all we are left with is the narrowness of our arrogance.

In truth, religion should go beyond tolerating critical views to welcoming them. Chris Lim's openness to what he doesn't know has only been an enlightening and enlivening force in his life, and faith can be similarly enlightened.

As a culture and a faith, we are awash in complex questions that deserve something more than bumper-sticker sloganeering. I know plenty of things the Bible "says" about, say, the cleansing of lepers or the ritual sacrifice of a goat, but that doesn't really settle much. What does it "say" about stem-cell research, nuclear power, gay marriage, cloning, global warming, racism, atomic weapons, the inequality of the sexes, rationed health care, immigration reform, or the economic disparity between the haves and the have-nots?

The truth is that the Bible *does* address these and other issues because it speaks to all issues moral and spiritual, but not by cheap proof-texting. If we are to be as serious as the problems we face, we will do well to remember that it's not enough to parrot ancient phrases at our convenience while ignoring the inconvenient ones. We must plumb the depths and embrace the mysteries of the revealed Word; we must study, interpret, and discern the hidden meaning that may speak to us only in, as Abraham Heschel puts it, "a whisper of a whisper of a hint."

In short, we must revere the gift of learning, even when it means *un*learning childish certitudes we have long outgrown. Like a pianist willing to work his craft for long hours at a time only to be told he must tear it all down and start again, the vitality of faith must not be divorced from the sanctity of learning.

## Questions for Discussion

1. Discuss the Henry Adams quote at the beginning of this chapter. From an emotional, intellectual, spiritual, and psychological standpoint, what does it mean to know *how* to learn?

2. Does Lim's youth come through to you? Or does he present as a preternaturally wise man? What is the difference between the accrual of information and the formation of wisdom?

3. At one point Lim talks about learning as a process by which we need not only to "gather in . . . but toss out" as well. What are some of the obstacles to "unlearning" old, cherished beliefs? Have you had to surrender such beliefs?

# Iconoclasts

# Chapter 8

# FRED NEWMAN

## *The Storyteller*

*Hear the music inside yourself first, then release it.*
*That is a very "in the moment" experience.*
—Fred Newman

WHEN I FIRST MET FRED NEWMAN SOME YEARS AGO, IT DIDN'T
take long to realize that his line of work made him the envy
of every six-year-old he'd ever come across, including my own
daughter. Fred is in the business of noise: not muffling it, but
making it. His vocal chords are a veritable fun house of gorks,
spluds, wheezes, nerks, and spizzles. By his own admission,
when he was a child, "I was unceremoniously removed from
several classrooms, once by my bottom lip."

A former Mouseketeer and Muppeteer and a regular on
the acclaimed radio show *A Prairie Home Companion*, in one
minute Fred can be heard replicating the sound of a church
organ as it plays the opening notes of a Bach "Magnificat,"
and in the next minute a vacuum cleaner as it sucks up a pile
of spilled pennies off a terrazzo floor. So I found it intriguing
that when I first came to interview him for this chapter, his
immediate response was to sit in stone silence at his dining
room table, his gangly arms crossed across his chest; his head,

with its thick shock of unruly white hair, was tilted slightly back, and his baby-blue eyes closed tight.

Only after a few minutes did he break his silence. "What do I hold sacred?" he begins, the last hints of his Georgia upbringing still detectable in a muted drawl that makes "I" come out more like "ah." "Well, I want to say that what I hold sacred is communication, but there's so much misunderstanding around that word. So much oversimplification and cliché." The sound guy was at a loss for words, but not for long. Over the course of a few hours, he would give communication its due as a vessel of the sacred, deftly breaking it down into three essential components: disposition, form, and content. While it's a tale elliptically told, Fred rewards your patience.

## DISPOSITION

Fred begins with the almost professorial observation that communication begins with a disposition of three essential elements: silence, stillness, and attentiveness. Then he tells me a story that is pivotal for him, for his development as a human being and as a professional noisemaker—a story that has to do with silence.

"I'm a pasty-faced little four-year-old kid growing up in tiny LaGrange, Georgia. And I'm a real antsy, squirrelly sort of boy." Like a June bug in a jelly jar, "I just can't sit still, always darting around. We're at my grandparents' house, and my grandfather, who was not a very touchy-feely sort of guy, calls me over in the back of the house and has me sit down in his big, floppy lap. The lap envelops me, but I'm still fidgety. Granddad simply holds me, puts his finger to his lips, and says, 'Shhh, just sit still and listen.' I get quiet, and I hear the wind, and in my typically impulsive way, I start to tell him this. But he silences me again, gently and lovingly. 'Shhhh, just listen.' And so I do. Slowly, fitfully, the fidgets give way to calm, and

I begin to settle down, deeper and deeper into the big floppy lap, and finally I get what he means. I just listen.

"The wind rustling through the oak trees makes a distinct sound, and my granddad quietly imitates it. The pine trees make another, and he softly rubs his hands together to imitate that as well." Fred uses his unique talents to simulate the sound of wind blowing through evergreens, then turns quiet. His eyes close again, lost in the thought of the pivotal moment lived some fifty years ago, as a tear gathers.

"Granddaddy knew I had a hard time sitting still," he tells me, with a clutch in his throat. "So he used this little session to teach me to do just that. To listen, to be quiet, and to simply be attentive to all the sounds around me. And here's the thing about that: You cannot listen without being *in the moment*" (his emphasis). The thing that he learned on his granddaddy's knee that afternoon, he tells me, is that in order to listen, he had to be still. This twitchy, antsy ADHD kid had to be still in order to listen. So when you *do* listen, when you *truly* listen, he went on, you are fully present in the moment. "You're not thinking about yesterday, or ten minutes ago," or where you left your slingshot, or grandma's pie cooling in the kitchen. You're in the moment. And that's all there is, isn't there? The moment. Now. It's kind of a discipline, he is suggesting, to be obedient to the sacred moment and not pass over it. It is what the physician-turned-author Spencer Johnson dubbed "The Precious Present."

With that observation, I mention to Fred how, when using traditional wedding vows, many newlyweds opt to "love, honor, and cherish" but not "obey" their mate, thinking the word carries the weight of servitude with it. But "obey" is actually derived from the Latin *oboedire*, which originally meant "to listen to." It was an ancient recognition that for two people to truly love one another, they had to also hear one another.

"I see the connection," he tells me. "I try to live my life [in conjunction with the idea of listening so that I am obedient to what] is happening around me; not what just happened or what once happened or what might happen, but what is happening." Fred's voice drops to just above a whisper. "Every once in a while my kids will see me just sitting very quietly, maybe in a rocking chair, rocking. 'Dad's just listening,' they'll say; 'Dad's doin' his work.'

"Once I wrote a poem with these lines," which he quoted:

Every whisper, every roar,
Every taste, touch, or tear,
Every moment . . .
is worship.

We pause for a bit, because I can tell that something is on Fred's mind. Hand on chin, eyes skyward (or at least ceiling-ward), he says to no one in particular, "Every moment is worship. We don't sit still and listen anymore. Conversation is a lost art." He is right; people speak in sound bites and don't so much listen to the other person as wait, often impatiently, for their turn to be heard. Earphones sequester us in our own world of sound. "We're barraged with electronic messages, texts, twitters, e-mails, voice mails, all under the guise of communication," he observes, "but we're not communicating." We're asking someone how they're doing, and at the same time we're checking our watch and walking away. No silence. No stillness. No communication. It separates us from one another, isolates us. That's not what God wants, for us to be isolated like that. In Fred's estimation this is the kind of thing that tears at the heart of community, makes community impossible.

"Imagine if the crowd that gathered to hear the Sermon on the Mount was preoccupied with other things," I say to Fred, and we bounce around a few ideas. "Imagine the ones half-listening, half-thinking, 'How long is this gonna go on? I really need to get dinner on the table.' Or, 'I wonder where Ben got those sandals he's wearing? I'd really like to get me a pair? Oh, what was that he just said about going the extra mile? I missed that.'"

"When you try to be in two places at once, in your head," Fred tells me, "you wind up being in neither." Then he goes on to tell me, in story form, what it means to be present even in the most unremarkable of moments, and how rewarding it can be:

"I remember a time years ago, back in the 1970s, when I was trying to make a living as a traveling carpet salesman. I'm driving my big old company station wagon [he does a dead-on imitation of the old V-8 engine] through the Arbuckle Mountains in southern Oklahoma, and I am just this side of nowhere. It's hot as blazes, and I'm thirsty, and I come upon an old filling station, with an equally old and weathered-looking guy sitting out front. I get outta my car and say to the guy, 'How ya doin'?' and he answers me in this slow Western twang [which Fred also re-creates to perfection] 'Ohhhhh . . . purty good, . . . considerin'.'

"Now, maybe because of my grandfather's instructions when I was a four-year-old, I heard that buried pause in his voice. I was attentive, still, and in the moment. And that's why I heard the 'considerin'.' I also couldn't help but notice that his face was scarred somethin' awful: cuts and scrapes from forehead to chin. So I asked him, 'Considerin' what?' And with that the old guy breaks into what had to be a ten-minute tale of midnight mayhem in his backyard the night before, about how he was half drunk when he heard commotion out back, only to find some critter prowling around in his trash cans, then leaping out at him as much in fear as in fury, how it fixed itself to his face, skittered down into his pants, scratched the hell out of him while he's running all over the yard, dogs barking and lights going on all over town. As he recounts this, Fred can't stop laughing at the memory, now over thirty years old, of a tall tale told by an old man he'd never met before, whose company he shared for no more than five minutes, and whom he would never see again.

"It was a priceless moment; the guy was a born storyteller, and he milked it for everything it was worth. I never would've heard it if I hadn't heard the *considerin'*—which I wouldn't have heard if I'd not been attentive—but even to this day, all these years later, it gets ahold of me."

The moral of Fred's little vignette recalled to mind a more somber one told about the eminent psychiatrist and Holocaust survivor Viktor Frankl. Late one night Frankl received a call from a distraught woman, a complete stranger, who was about to commit suicide but decided to randomly call one more doctor in hopes that her despair could be lifted. Frankl managed to keep the woman on the phone for about an hour or so, and he got her to agree to come to his office the next morning.

The next day he had no idea whether she would show up or whether she was even alive. When she did arrive, he was elated and asked her what it was he had said the night before that gave her the will to stay alive. "It was nothing you said," she told him. "It was simply the fact that in the dead of night a complete stranger was willing to keep company with me that gave me cause for hope."

Silence, stillness, attentiveness to the here and now; attentiveness to the other, whether evidenced in a tale such as Fred's that borders on the ludicrous or in a dramatic moment such as Frankl's that juggles life and death—these are all very much glimpses of that which is holy. We'd be hard-pressed to call Fred's moment with the old man at the gas station a spiritual awakening, but it was for both of them a rich experience that only happened because one man took another man seriously. He met the man as his grandfather would have him meet the man: He listened to the stranger, heard the hint that was buried in the pause, and invited the man to tell his story. In that way, however briefly, two strangers connected with one another, and so for that moment they no longer were strangers. And that *is* a spiritual awakening. "Be still, and know that I am God," says God via the psalmist (Ps. 46:10), who implores his readers to listen for the word of a God who is best heard in faint whisper and subtle hint, the wind in the evergreens, the buried pause.

## FORM

For Fred, the communication tool of choice is the well-told tale. "I know that there are a whole lot of different ways we communicate with one another and with the world, but because I am a 'sound guy,' and more important, because of where I grew up, in the deep South, storytelling is in my blood; it has always come as easily to me as breathing or bike riding." I ask him to elaborate on what it was about the South that made storytelling so important.

"Let me explain LaGrange, Georgia in the 1950s," he begins. "It's a small town, and like just about everywhere in the South at that time, it's a racially and economically segregated town. There's a road in LaGrange called Country Club Road, and if you go out Country Club, you come to the homes of the wealthier folks, mostly upper-middle-class professionals. All white. But down near where the road begins, there's a small section called Red Line Alley. Red Line Alley is a series of shacks that at one time were slave quarters and now, in my childhood, still housed black families.

"On the corner, where the two roads meet, is Fling's Country Store, run by a guy named Jack Fling; a huge man, a white guy, with a big head and a nose like a hood ornament. Now, Jack was a storyteller, and I remember going in there one day in the heat of the summer, with the fans on and pushing a lot of hot air around, to buy myself one of those two-sticked orange-flavored popsicles. I'm an ugly little kid—glasses, skinny, pallid-white skin, freckles, snaggly teeth—of about ten or eleven, wearing nothing but a cheap pair of shorts with an elastic waistband. After Jack gives me my popsicle, he sits me on a Coke carton and says to me in his deep drawl, 'Fraid, did ah eva tell ya 'bout that big ol' cat o' mahn?' Then he proceeds to tell me this great, grand, nonsensical story about how this cat he owned always thought he was the biggest, baddest animal in the house until the day Jack got fed up with its arrogance, put it in his Chrysler, drove it down to the circus, held that cat's face up to the lions and tigers, and told it, 'Now *those* are big cats!' He swore that from that day forward, that cat was the picture of humility.

Of course, when Jack told Fred the tale, it had a lot more window dressing and digressions and flourishes, and by the time Jack was done regaling him and he was done laughing, Fred looked down to the floor. At his feet was a pool of melted orange popsicle, and in his hand were two empty sticks. Now *that's* communicating!

"But there's more to my memory, because what made storytelling so important wasn't Jack Fling, it was his store, and here's why: Because of where it was situated, Fling's was one of the few places frequented by both blacks and whites, and the two races mixed socially there: if nowhere else in LaGrange, we mixed there. And when one person had a story to tell, everyone would listen. It didn't matter if it was the white attorney from up on the hill or the black yard worker from Red Line Alley who spent the day cutting that attorney's lawn. For some reason everyone was everyone's equal in that store, especially when it was time to tell or listen to a story. Everyone's word was met with the same respect.

"I think at heart we somehow understood that every human being has a story to tell, has *their* story, and it's worth hearing." From here Fred and I go on to reflect on the sacred nature of storytelling, about how so many of the lessons of the Scriptures in any religious tradition are embedded in stories whose worth relies less on historical accuracy than on ineluctable wisdom. We speak of how the temptation of Adam is really a meditation on hubris, how the story of Ruth speaks to our capacity for kindness and God's capacity for mercy, and how the tragic flaw in Judas is emblematic of every person's reluctance to accept God's grace.

Fred then explains to me how, for a kid growing up in the segregated South, it was a holy experience, because it carried people above their differences to a place where they were all kin. "I learned a lot of great mouth sounds from those storytellers—the sound of water dripping from a roof, a dog barking, a helicopter hovering (he demonstrates each in turn)—and a lot of great lessons."

## CONTENT

Complementing form and disposition in this holy trinity of talk was content. What Fred gleaned from his upbringing in Georgia was that a lot of what he referred to as the sacred act of communication came to him on two different levels, from two different sources, with two very different kinds of content. Thus Fred refers to the content of the head, and also the content of the heart.

Fred was a kid born into an extremely reserved, extremely white middle-class Presbyterian family. Lots of regimentation, discipline, caution, stifling of feelings, self-denial. Things like reading and thinking and discussion and schoolwork and grades were very, very important—the content of the head—and he came to respect that. But the person most responsible for raising him, probably the most influential person in his young life, was a housekeeper named Dot, who was black and who set a notably different tone for him.

"Dot wasn't classically educated, but she was extremely wise, and I trusted her. I remember a time in my early years, when I was about six or seven. I'd been acting up a little, hyperactive as always, chafing at the constraints my mother put on me. When we were alone one day, Dot looked me in the eye and said, 'Now, Fred, you do what your mama tells you to do because she's your mama.' Then she paused a moment and added, just as emphatically, 'But don't always listen to what she *says*, because sometimes she talks trash!'" It was not only a bold statement; it was also a brilliant one. On the one hand she was reminding Fred that a child has to obey his parent, but on the other hand she was telling him that from where she sat, she could see the foibles and the foolishness that people of privilege were capable of. It was Dot's way of saying, "Fred, there's a whole other world that you don't even know about."

"I took that sentiment seriously; I wanted to know about that other world. I started going over to Dot's home, where she would continue to look out for me." Whereas Fred's family taught caution, she encouraged him to be bold and to explore the things that made him curious, and so he did. They also confided many secrets in one another, precisely *because* they trusted one another. "I remember the time I saw a white man push himself past a group of black kids to take a sip of water at the 'colored only' water fountain at the town courthouse," Fred recalls. "When it upset me so, my parents told me that that's just the way things are, but when I told Dot about it, her take was very different. 'That's wrong. That's just wrong,' she told me, and she didn't have to elaborate. The incident reminded me, and probably her, how, when Dot would take me to the Rexall, I could sit at the counter but she couldn't.'" (Ubiquitous in the 1950s and

'60s, Rexall was a neighborhood drugstore, often with a lunch counter. In 1964, when the Civil Rights Act was passed and the lunch counter was integrated, Fred asked for and was given the "Whites Only" sign that had hung behind the counter; he still has it.) "All the slights I saw Dot endure reminded me of what she had said about my mother; the person in charge has to be heeded because they're in charge, but sometimes they're just talking trash." Such was the content of the heart.

Fred believes it was because of the time he spent with Dot in her home and in her neighborhood that he eventually started appreciating as many facets of the black culture that a white child of means in the segregated South of the 1950s could possibly grasp. "It was there that I gained a deeper regard for the indignities endured by Dot and her family and other black families, and of how they coped with those indignities. It was also there that I got my first exposure to the blues and its poetry, how the music re-created the rhythmic sounds of cotton field or the rock splitters. Black men laboring for white landowners. I also got my first taste of the black church and a style of worship that was decidedly different from my own because it was all about lament and liberation. I saw how through art and worship the community gave voice to both their oppression and their determination to overcome it.

"As much as my culture communicated through the mind—think of the predictable Presbyterian three-point sermon, week after week—the black culture communicated through the soul. And when I think of why I so deeply value communication, I think of these two components and how indispensable they both are." Head and heart. Science and art. The laws of Leviticus and the poetry of the Psalms.

We speak a bit about the God of the Scriptures as exemplifying both spirit and wisdom, and Fred agrees that for his money, this is the right synthesis. A wise God but also a God of passion, who calls us to be both as well.

## FROM COMMUNICATION TO COMMUNION

True to form, when he wants to get at the grist of what he is saying, Fred tells a tale. "Let me tell you a story that gets at *how* communication is so sacred to me," he begins.

"[The cellist] Yo-Yo Ma was the guest performer on *A Prairie Home Companion* one night, and I was coming off stage after doing some sort of skit that involved a whole lot of mouth sounds and impersonations and stuff. Ma comes up behind me, grabs me, gives me a big, generous, enthusiastic hug, and says to me, 'How do you do that? How do you make those sounds?'

"Pointing to my ear, and then to his, I smiled and said to him, '*You* know how I do it,' and he immediately understood what I meant. 'Yes, I do. You listen!' And that's exactly what I meant." You get still, Fred is saying. You stay in the moment, and you listen. You listen to the sound of the leaves in your granddaddy's backyard, or the story that old man Fling has to tell, or the insights Dot doles out, or the doleful harmonica of an old blues musician.

But to hear Fred tell it, you do more than that. You let those experiences come into you and penetrate your very soul. You absorb it until it's a part of you. And then you feed it back, whether through a cello or a sermon or a story or a bunch of mouth sounds: it comes out of you as if it were a part of you. And when you're there to offer it and someone else is there to receive it, with the two of you in that moment, giving and receiving, one of you sharing a piece of your story, your own self, and the other sitting as rapturous as a little kid whose popsicle is melting and he doesn't even realize it—now *that's* communication.

I call to mind a passage from the poet Rainer Maria Rilke and recite a portion of it for Fred. Rilke speaks of all a poet must take in and internalize before being able to utter so much as one verse of poetry:

> For the sake of a single verse . . . One must be able to think back to days of childhood that are still unexplained, . . . to days in rooms withdrawn and quiet and to mornings by the sea, to the sea itself, to seas, to nights of travel that rushed along on high and flew with all the stars. . . . And still it is not enough to have memories. One must be able to forget them when they are many, and one must have the great patience to wait until they come again. For it is not yet the memories themselves. Not till they have turned to blood within us, to glance, and gesture, nameless, and no longer to be distinguished from ourselves—not till then can it happen that in a most rare hour the first word of a verse arises in their midst and goes forth from them.
>
> (*The Notebooks of Malte Laurids Brigge*)

Fred silently nods his agreement. "That's it!" he says.

We've been sitting at his dining room table for some time now, and we're ready to call it a day. With a kind of understated reverence, Fred places his hands on the table, an old, weathered, barn-board table that he and his wife have had for over thirty years. Lots of nicks and deep-sunk stains, like impromptu sculptings, graffiti, and frescoes memorializing celebrated moments long past. "We've had a lot of meals over the years at this table, with a lot of different people and a lot of different circumstances, in our lives and in theirs." He thinks of the stories that were told here, the ideas that were swapped, the fevered debates and passionate discussions. He thinks of the time when he was privileged to have Dot come north to visit and share a meal here. Those meals have always been special to him, he tells me, and he thinks it has to do with everything we've been talking about this afternoon. "Speaking and listening, sharing your heart and being in the moment with people you love," he says. "Communication."

Fred thinks for a minute, as still and quiet as he was when I first entered. And then he adds, "Not just communication. Communion."

As we say in church, the table is prepared for us. Let us keep the feast.

## THE SACRED WORD

What emerged from Fred's thoughts about the sacredness of communication was theology in the guise of folktale. The story of the old man with the scarred face, the one who was doing "purty good . . . considerin'," is really an account of what it means to have sufficient reverence for the other that when you ask about his welfare, you do so with genuine concern, even when he is a stranger. The level playing field of Fling's General Store, where the inequities of station or race were, if only for a moment, irrelevant to the telling of a good yarn, was an exercise in dignity and a taste of what Martin Luther King identified as "the blessed community." In a similar manner the white man's pushing forward to drink from the "colored only" fountain was arrogance born of ignorance, just as Dot's declaiming his actions as "just not right" was a reminder that, as Paul wrote to the Galatians, in God's economy there is "neither Jew nor Greek, . . . neither slave nor free, . . . for you are all one in Christ Jesus" (Gal. 3:28).

And when I imagine an old man of good Presbyterian reserve, never himself touchy-feely, scooping his fidgety, four-year-old grandson into his ample lap and teaching the boy to be prayerfully still so that he could absorb the natural wonders in their midst, I cannot think of it as anything less than divine love in human form. For how better does God come to us but through acts of generosity and kindness that we perform for one another, perhaps only more so when we must step out of character in order to perform them?

◦✕◦

Perhaps a hint to the sacred power of "communication" lies in the fact that the word itself is cognate with "common," which comes to us from the French *commun*, often meaning "shared burdens." It is also the word from which we get our term "community."

To share our burdens. This is what Viktor Frankl did when he stayed on the phone in the dead of night with a complete stranger who otherwise might have ended her life. And though less dramatically (and even with a soupçon of humor), it is what Fred Newman did when he invited the leathered old Oklahoman with the scraped face to tell the fantastic tale of how a mysterious beast set upon his trash cans, his drunken head, and even down the front of his pants. And what did Fred's grandfather do but unburden his squirrelly grandson of the inveterate fidgetiness that kept the boy from learning how to listen?

In each of these moments there is a wisp of the sacred because something is given, something is received, something is taught, and something is learned. Isolation is bested; the light shines in the darkness. But more than that—and this, I think, is the real beauty of communication—in each instance the roles are reversible.

Frankl may have given a woman her second chance, but he also received from her a lesson he would carry with him throughout his career and to the very end of his life: it is not only what you know that can help another; it is also that you are willing, as were Job's friends, to simply sit in shared sorrow. Fred was deliriously happy to hear the old cowboy's tale of the beast in the night, but the opposite can be intuited as well, that a man who passes his days in solitude, who lives alone in the middle of nowhere, might have his tedium broken by a complete stranger who cared enough to tease out of him a story that no one else gave a second thought to. And while Grandpa Newman gave his grandson the gift of quiet, what greater pleasure could he have derived than to have the youngster nestle into that floppy lap in all of the unself-consciousness with which little children are singularly blessed? Whatever burdens age brought to Grandpa were surely lifted, if only momentarily, as he savored this instant that spanned the generations.

Sharing burdens lightens them, just as sharing joys multiplies them, and aren't these two sides to the same coin of communication? This is the way I think of the rite of holy communion: sacred sharing. It is the gesture in which hopes and sadnesses, joys and burdens intermingle. Where broken body and spilled blood become the things that save us from the hell of our own dark and endless nights. For around that table, be we bankers or beggars, saints or sinners, people of great name or no estate, the cup is common. The need is identical. The gift is incalculable. The story that must be told. It is our story, yours and mine. All of ours. Mary was common enough to have given it birth. Jesus was common enough to have brought it to its inevitable conclusion. We are common enough to continue to tell it—and to live it.

## Questions for Discussion

1. What role can storytelling play in preserving a community's memory in a manner that is different from a historical chronicle? Can a truth be conveyed ahistorically?
2. How is the notion of communication made sacred by Fred's story about Yo-Yo Ma?
3. In this chapter, how does the dining room table serve as a symbol of something more than simply a place to eat? Discuss ways in which everyday objects in your own life point to something greater than their stated use.

# Chapter 9

# TAO PORCHON-LYNCH
## *The Tao of Tao*

*What would I save? What comes to mind
is everything. And nothing.*
—Tao Porchon-Lynch

TAO PORCHON-LYNCH WAS PERHAPS THE MOST DIFFICULT INTER-
view I conducted for this book, not because there is anything
opaque or even reticent about her but because she proved to
be so *physically* elusive. If one week she was conducting a yoga
workshop in England, the next she would be on retreat at an
ashram in Delhi, India. After that it would be back to the
States with an itinerary filled either with lectures, interviews,
writing, competitive ballroom dancing, or all of the above.
Through it all, it was easy to forget that the person I was chas-
ing like a dragonfly through the deep woods was ninety-three
years old.

She is a little sprite of a woman, who at a distance looks
as though a stiff breeze could knock her over. It is only on
closer inspection that you see the understated strength etched
in her lean, lithe, sinewy body. Her years of practicing yoga
have been very good to her. (She reports beginning the practice when she was eight years old and, eighty-five years in,

still refers to herself as "a beginner.") When so many others her age or younger have trouble walking two steps without a wheeze, Tao looks like she could run a seven-minute mile without breaking a sweat. Perhaps this explains why she not only enters those dance contests (with partners often in their twenties), she wins them.

Her mind is no less supple or durable. Though she speaks slowly, with words that are whisper-soft, she dispenses wisdom with crystal clarity and timeless insight. In recollecting past events, some from her early childhood, she does not hold forth with the vague generality of a cracker-barrel raconteur but with the encyclopedic detail of a college physics professor. And when she tells me just what she would rescue from her fire, her words are delivered with transparency and conviction.

"What I cherish most in life is the ability to find value in everything," she tells me. "I don't clutter my mind with negative thoughts, only positive ones. Something good can be drawn from any calamity. We are all made from the same dust, nothing lasts, but everything has value."

Such optimism can easily be misconstrued as the simple musings of a soft mind, a kind of "If life gives you lemons . . ." bromide that fails to account for the struggles and equivocations with which even the most sheltered of lives must cope. But anyone who makes that criticism of Tao fails to appreciate both the thought and the history that lie behind it.

## ONE IN THE SPIRIT

While Tao believes that "all religions are paths to God," she aligns herself with Vedantism, a philosophical arm of Hinduism—linked to the sacred Hindu texts, the Upanishads—that stresses the pursuit of truth through daily meditation and governed by a loving morality. No newcomer or faddist, Tao has studied this form of Hinduism throughout her adult life, including tutelage under esteemed Eastern teachers Indra Devi (dubbed "the First Lady of Yoga," she held that honorific until her death in 2002 at the age of 102) and Sri Aurobindo (a philosopher who introduced the concept of spiritual evolution into Vedantic thought). When Tao speaks of yogic meditation, she does so with care and patience drawn from years of study, the synthesis of thought and practice crystallizing with each sentence.

"The word 'yoga' comes from the Sanskrit *yug*," she informs me, "which means unity of body, mind, and spirit." Aware of the deceptive simplicity of this idea, she pauses for a moment for my sake, so that it might sink in. As she then further explains, *yug* also implies the unity of all creation. In Tao's credo, yoga invites her to feel both personally integrated and also integrated into the world at large. In her own words, through yogic meditation "I can look within myself, then look at other people, and realize that all of us, right down to the tiniest insect, all beat with the same heartbeat. Life is within us, around us, and through us." Thus it is that she can find value in everything.

When she speaks of this unity, I am reminded of the words of the ancient rabbi Hillel, who said in describing the Torah, "That which is hateful to you, do not do unto another: This is the whole Torah. The rest is commentary. Now go and study." What empathy is to Hillel, unity is to Tao; it is the single guiding essence of faith that is then amplified in the practice of that faith. For one, it is study; for another, meditation. For both, it is an exercise in living faith, a journey inward that then gives rise to the journey outward. Introspection that makes possible a moral life.

After she's confident that I have at least a layperson's grasp of the connection between the unity of all things and their intrinsic value, a kind of *Vedantism for Dummies*, Tao then pushes on to give a hint as to how her discipline and her mind-set contribute to both her sense of inner peace and her physical longevity. As a Vedantic *yogini* (the feminine counterpart of a yogi), it is for Tao no less a mental exercise than a physical one: "I don't clutter my mind with negative thoughts because negative thoughts are a symbol of decay. If I am thinking negatively, I am decaying myself; so in the midst of any disaster, amid anything that might trigger negative thoughts, I keep in mind that something good can come of it. I try never to let negative thoughts bring decay on my body." For Tao, to think negative thoughts is to wander down a perilous, booby-trapped dead-end road, a trail fraught with danger and devoid of anything good. It is not realism: it is masochism.

As Tao distills to me the beliefs she has gleaned from these many years of meditation, it strikes me that a thread of commonality weaves its way through her life and connects her vibrancy, her personal faith, and her social ethic. When she talks about how she has come to see a unity in the cosmos—human life as neither more nor less a part of the greater whole than the life of the smallest insect—she intimates the very Western religious idea that there is inherent worth in all things. God the Creator's creation is good. Put another way, the world doesn't have to be fractious (a Hindu view), *disin*tegrated (a Buddhist view), or fallen (a Jewish and Christian view). Instead, it can be whole, or made whole. Or if not, then at least it can be brought closer to wholeness than it is now. As Tao might put it, "That is the whole of the Upanishads. Now go and meditate!"

The reason yogic meditation is not solely an internal experience for Tao is because in finding a sense of wholeness within, she is at the same time seeing herself as nothing more nor less than a mirror image of what is possible for the world. In this way meditation affirms for her both her relationship *with* and her responsibility *to* the rest of creation. Though Eastern in derivation, her thinking has parallels in both Judaism and Christianity (By which I mean Eastern-based religions that predominate in the Western world). To Jews, the world is a fractious place of pain and sadness, which we can make whole only through acts of kindness. And to Christians, there is parallel thinking in the idea that in the Godhead incarnate in Jesus as the Christ, "we, though many, are one body" (Rom. 12:5).

## FROM WEST TO EAST TO WEST

Tao's embrace of Hinduism and its decidedly Eastern belief that everything is ephemeral was born out from the very start of her long life, when complications from her birth cost her mother *her* life. "Most of us aren't willing to face the reality of impermanence and death," said the Buddha. "That's because we forget that our lives are transitory." Having come into the world in a manner that does nothing if not underscore the transitory nature of life, Tao has never forgotten it. More to the point, even beyond the circumstances of her birth, she was the product of it.

Her father, a Frenchman, considered himself not equal to the task of raising a daughter by himself; so when he immigrated to Canada, he sent a very young Tao to be raised by his brother, a diplomat living in what was then the British colony of India. After never having known her mom, Tao would see her father only once, "in England, for no more than five minutes." She does not explain the circumstances of her encounter or tell me her age at the time, but she utters this brief declaration, not surprisingly, with neither bitterness nor sadness in her voice. (*"All conditioned things are impermanent,"* says the Dhammapada, one text of the Buddhist scriptures. *"When one sees this in wisdom, then one becomes dispassionate toward the painful."*)

She grew up in India. In short order, things got very interesting as it became clear to the young girl that her upbringing, like her birth, would be anything but conventional.

"I have a very clear recollection of being a little child and having an odd-looking native guy visiting our home," she recalls. "And I remember saying to my uncle, as young children will do without the veneer of propriety, 'Who was that funny-looking little man visiting my house?'

"'Don't call him a funny looking little man!' he scolded. 'This is a great man, a heroic man who may well die for his cause and not even care!' My uncle, you see, *always* believed in his friend Gandhi."

Her exposure to Gandhi was not confined to this one incident, nor did her uncle have just a casual acquaintance with the cause. Tao quickly came to understand her uncle to be a fierce supporter of Indian independence, who was marching with Gandhi well before many Indians were. By the early 1920s, so was Tao. "I went on marches until the late '20s, when the British started using violence against the protesters. That's when my uncle forbade me from going. He went on the Great Salt march, but I did not," she recalls, with just a trace of longing in her tone. (The Salt March, or Salt Satyagraha, began in March of 1930 and was a campaign of nonviolent protest against the British salt monopoly in colonial India. It is believed by many to be the single event that tipped the scales in favor of the Indians. In today's India, it has assumed proportions similar to our Boston Tea Party of 1773.)

But though prohibited from attending the marches, Tao was not cut off from the "funny little man" who remained a regular visitor to her home. Her recollections carry both personal warmth ("People used to get so exasperated with him because nothing seemed to faze him!") and prescience ("He told me that women should have the same freedoms as men"). To this day her home is still adorned with photographs and mementos of the time. When she tells me at a later date, "You know, I've never been afraid of death," it is as though she is echoing her uncle's observation made over eighty years earlier about the man they called the Mahatma. Tao is no newcomer to the Eastern thought of the yogis and Brahmins; though not born into a family of practitioners, she certainly grew up immersed in it.

Some years later, now a young woman, she returned to France, where, as global events shifted from India to the European front, life proved to be no less dramatic. World War II was breaking out, and Tao's aunt became a prominent member of the French Resistance. Perhaps in keeping with the Vedic prayer *"May we resolve to dedicate our lives to the service of humankind and uplift them to Divinity,"* Tao, now only twenty, became active in the cause as well. Though her memory bank may be well stocked with recollections of these years, she shares with me only a few, and does so sparely, with surprisingly little attention to detail:

"I remember once running to a local monastery and fetching a priest's outfit, a nun's habit, and clothes for two children, which we then used to help a family of four [Jews] escape France. I also remember watching the Germans torture a friend of mine when he got caught" participating in resistance activities. She pauses briefly, then adds, "There was also a time when I myself avoided being arrested by the Germans by getting away five minutes before they showed up." She doesn't expand on these memories, and I don't ask her to, sensing it would somehow be a violation of privacy if I did. She will give me what she chooses to give me, I think, and I will not press for more. *"Whatever I am offered,"* says the Bhagavad Gita, *"in devotion with a pure heart—a leaf, a flower, fruit, or water—I accept with joy."* Perhaps Tao's tao is contagious.

But just as her uncle protected her from the violence of the British in India, as things became increasingly precarious in France, her family made the decision to send her out of the country. Ironically, the place that offered her safest haven was England, the erstwhile enemy of Indian independence. Now just in her early twenties, Tao moved to London, not far from de Gaulle's headquarters in exile, where she found work as a nightclub dancer and earned enough money both to sustain herself and to send funds home in support of the resistance. She did this for the duration of the conflict.

The war years still sorely test her resolve "to find value and goodness in everything." After all, what earthly good can be extracted from the horrors of the Nazi Holocaust? And if there *was* any shred of good, could it possibly be deemed commensurate with the cost? On this count Tao has at best struck a note of resignation if not reconciliation. "There is always some good that we can find in the face of awful experiences," she tells me, adding as a caveat, "but that doesn't mean I am incapable of hating."

She goes on to intimate not only that there are horrors in life, but also that the kinds she has witnessed firsthand are such that she cannot deny how they have shaped her thinking. She came into the world at the end of the Great War and on the cusp of the Great Depression, with a birth that cost her mother her life. She was raised in a British colony teeming with poverty and resentment and in the throes of a bloody revolution. She not only experienced the deprivations and atrocities of the Second World War; she also risked her life for a cause that cost others theirs. She endured the assassination of her beloved Mahatma in 1948. All this by the time she was a mere thirty years old. To this we can add, if speculatively, the innumerable losses both natural and otherwise that accrue with living and with age: the death of family, the dissolution of friendships, the disenchantment that comes, as it does to all of us, when people we trust break our hearts.

But for Tao, this is precisely where her ability to find value in everything serves her so well, for in her own words, "Nothing is important in and of itself. What makes it important is where it takes me."

## EVIL IN THE FACE OF GOOD, AND VICE VERSA

This brings us back to what she might have learned from the atrocities she witnessed that has helped her to be a better yogini. "When I say that I don't want to spend time dwelling on things I might hate because negative thoughts can only bring decay to my body and soul," she tells me, reiterating her earlier sentiments, "I am speaking [not in a vacuum but] from personal experience. So instead of denying that there are things I might hate, which would be a lie, I simply learn to avoid them." This may sound like an intellectual feint, but instead I think it is indicative of a very nuanced understanding of evil in the face of good.

It would in fact be the height of naïveté and the epitome of repression for Tao to deny that terrible things happen, often arbitrarily, often for no reason, often to good people, or that there is intrinsic, equivalent value in everything that goes on in life. But that is not what she does. It is not her mind-set. Instead, by not dwelling on the things she might hate—the terrible, cruel, gratuitously destructive things, those booby traps in the road—she is refusing to cede to those forces, refusing to give those things power over her. Tao is not denying their existence; quite the opposite, she is affirming both their existence and their potential to do her harm, or in her words, bring decay upon her.

The effect of her mind-set is twofold, I think. First, it protects her from obsessing over evils she is powerless to correct; second, it gives her untrammeled room to find compassion for the victim without bearing hatred for the perpetrator.

Apropos of the first point, she once told me about an exchange she had with her personal physician that serves as something of an allegory. "She wanted me to come in for a physical, but I resisted, literally, for years. Yet I finally relented."

"What made you relent?" I asked.

"I went to see her on one condition," she tells me, a mischievous, conspiratorial grin crossing her face. "I told her that if she finds anything terribly wrong with me, she's not to say anything. Not a word. I don't want to know. But if she finds nothing wrong, she can talk. She can tell me how healthy I am."

"So how'd it go?"

"She examined me pretty thoroughly. Then, after the physical, we talked, and talked and talked!"

As to the second point, we have to understand that for Tao, yoga is much more than a physical exercise: it is an exercise in compassion. Tao believes that yoga can be a healing experience for individuals and, by extension, for the whole world. "A guiding principle in my life and in my practice," she says, "is to try to understand that which is within me and why I am here. I am not here to fight everyone I meet. Instead, through yoga, I come to realize again and again that we all pulsate with the same heartbeat." As her beloved uncle once instructed her, "Never ask anyone to understand you; always try to understand them."

I notice this notion of healing to be a recurring theme in our conversations. Tao speaks a lot about "wholeness," of course, both of the individual and of the world. It is no mistake, I think, that the words "whole" and "health" both derive from the same Old English word *hælan* (from *hāl*), meaning "to make whole, sound, or well." Nor is by accident that this pillar of her thought is the exact opposite of "decay," another word that comes up with some frequency for her. "*All differences in this world,*" said Swami Vivekananda, "*are of degree and not of kind, because oneness is the secret of everything.*"

## KEEP IT SIMPLE

There is a beguiling paradox in many strands of Hinduism, of which Vedantism is an integral part. The scriptures and teachings are dense and complex. (The Bhagavad Gita alone, one of over twenty sacred Hindu texts, runs to over 900 pages.) They are rich with symbolism, in many instances requiring great intellect to parse their meaning with clarity and accuracy. And yet for the practitioner such as Tao, all of that complexity derives from the one fundamental, irreducible, and extremely simple belief in the unity of the cosmos and all that that implies.

This paradox of simplicity in complexity is symbolized in the most charming of manners in Tao's home. Her modest accommodations are, in her own words, "cluttered with a lifetime of mementos" that speak not only to the longevity of that life but also to *its* richness and complexity. It is here that one sees token reminders of her many relationships—from the pacifist Gandhi to the warrior de Gaulle, from a sax-blowing President Clinton to an ivory-tickling Duke Ellington—and her many experiences. But the clutter too can be distilled, clarified, and simplified, for she speaks about it with the same synthesis with which she speaks about her yogic commitment to the unity of the world: "None of this [stuff] is important in and of itself," she observes. "The only thing that's important is where it takes me in my memory."

Where it takes her. Still on the move. Still traveling, lecturing, meditating, listening, dancing. Still endeavoring to find the value in everything and to impart that value to others. And at ninety-three and counting, still, as she puts it, "a beginner." On a journey to wholeness that has no end. It is a point she makes manifest for me when, while reflecting on the ineradicable scar World War II left on her heart and the need to avoid those things that decay the mind with hatred, she confesses to me, "I still have a hard time accepting a ride in a Volkswagen."

Tao's belief in the intrinsic value of all things is a close cousin to the Judeo-Christian concept of grace, and here's how:

As the Rabbi Arthur Waskow taught us in an earlier chapter, Biblical teaching points out that God is a Creator God (thus Genesis introduces us to God), whose creation comes to life as the Spirit/wind of God (*ruakh Elohim*, Gen. 1:2) blows over it and God breathes life (*nefesh khayyah*, "breath of life"; 1:30; 2:7) into "every living thing that moves" (1:28). At the end of a day of creation, God beholds what God has created and typically (seven times) declares "*ki-tov*," "It is good."

From this little passage we glean three things: All that is exists because of God. All that is receives life from God. And all that is fundamentally is essentially good. Or as Tao put it, "all of us . . . beat with the same heartbeat."

We are all of God, whose breath brings us life. By extension, we, from the most estimable human being to the tiniest insect, are inherently good (*ki tov*). But this goodness is not earned: it is bestowed. As Martin Luther pointed out, we are not worthy by virtue of the deeds we do, however noble, or unworthy by the sins we commit, however heinous. We are worthy, valuable, good, by virtue of the fact that God has called us into being, has breathed life into us. By our essence.

Grace is unmerited love—love not only *because* of who we are but also *despite* who we are. It is divinely bestowed, irrevocably granted, and impossible to repay. It is the love that God felt for Adam and Eve even as they were banished from the garden. Grace is why, according to the Talmud, when Egyptian forces were swallowed up as the temporarily parted Red Sea waters closed in over them, God wept. And it is why the tragedy of Judas was not that he ransomed Jesus for thirty dollars but that Judas could not bring himself to receive the forgiveness that was assured him the very next afternoon, when Christ died on the cross.

To shift our thoughts from a celestial level to an earthly one, what matters most in our lives is not so much divine grace but human willingness to channel that grace in our interactions with one another and with the world. How do we confirm the inherent value of all people? How do we love those we don't like, those who have done us harm, those from whom our kindness is met with indifference? It is a simple question that lacks a simple answer, but perhaps we can start by believing that the unmerited love that God holds for us is neither greater nor lesser than that which God holds for all that God has breathed life into.

It is just a beginning. But then, as with Tao when she told me that after eighty-five years of practicing yoga, she is still a beginner, we are all always just beginning.

## Questions for Discussion

1. What does Tao mean when she says, "Nothing lasts, but everything has value"?
2. Using Tao's life as a backdrop, discuss how negative thoughts can be injurious to us.
3. Reflect on the Vedic prayer cited above: *"May we resolve to dedicate our lives to the service of humankind and uplift them to Divinity."* How, in your own faith tradition, can service to humankind be understood as a gift to the Divine?

# Chapter 10

## CATHRINE KELLISON

### *The Little Black Box*

*I was educated more by the streets than by the schools.*
—Cathrine Kellison

CATHRINE KELLISON IS A WOMAN OF INFORMAL ELEGANCE, TALL and trim, with alabaster skin that belies her sixty-three years and a warm smile that softens her beautiful, steely blue eyes. Easily one of the most popular members of the media studies faculty at New York University, one does not take up her time so much as share it, primarily with a swirl of students calling on the phone, breezing in and out of her home office, or buttonholing her with a question about a recent assignment, an upcoming exam, a parsed participle, or what to wear on a big date. And to all, she obliges, not only willingly but also gracefully. If this steady flow of young minds into her study is any indication, Cathrine's worth to her department is inestimable, which is not a bad measure of accomplishment for someone who does not even hold a high school diploma.

"An awful lot of my educational trail can be found in what I call my little black box," she tells me. "Like that box on airplanes that contains all the information, all the history of the flight. Mine's actually a kind of portable metal crate with a bunch of tiny compartments, and it's where I keep what I call my 'tangible intangibles': letters, notes, doodles, articles, poetry, random thoughts gathered over the years, many contained in journals. Most of the thoughts are mine, but many more are contributed by people who have come in and out of my life. The history of my flight, if you will." She takes me on a tour.

"Here are my journals," she tells me as she opens up one compartment of a black metal box that is about the size of a two-drawer filing cabinet. It is filled with notebooks of various sizes, styles, dates, and decorations; one has a blank cover, another a glued-on cover from an old telephone book, another a Beatles collage (perhaps homage to the morning many years ago when, while staying at a friend's house in London, Cathrine was awakened by the sound of a young Paul McCartney downstairs noodling out a tune he would later call "Blackbird"). "I've always kept at least one notebook out on a coffee table at all times so anyone who's so inspired can jot down whatever they please. There are a lot of thoughts from a lot of people crammed into these pages. Friends, acquaintances, and even strangers would pick them up, draw in them, leave little notes. A kind of communal muse." And then she adds, almost as an afterthought, "Or maybe it's my life as an open book."

Sliding open another compartment, I expect to see a trove of inspired artwork or poetry or talismans of some sort but instead find a bundle of old bills, deeds, and other official-looking documents.

"This is my 'grown-up' compartment. It keeps me mindful of the fact that, as playful as life can be, there are rents to pay and responsibilities to be met and noses to be wiped, and I take that all quite seriously." In another drawer is a pile of about twenty or so small notepads, her "portable journals," that she packs when she's in transit to capture observations she might otherwise forget if she waited until she returned home to record them, and in yet another are stacks of screenplays she long ago collaborated on.

The last compartment, the only one under lock and key, "is my not-so-grown-up drawer, where I keep a little stash of pot," she tells me unabashedly. "Loosens the creative writing synapses, ya know."

## A TREASURE CHEST

There is good reason why this little black box is Cathrine's answer to the question of what it is she so dearly values in her life. "I've had an awful lot of adventures in my time," she reports: "world travel, fascinating characters, trying circumstances. But I've always had my antenna up, always paid attention to what was going on around me. Always kept notes, mental or otherwise. Always kept my chronicles, my scriptures, if you will. That's been my education."

When I ask her about the content of that education, about what wisdom she's recorded in those journals and notepads and the like, she thinks long and hard before answering: "In really broad brush strokes, I've learned two things. First, I've learned how to read people, how to know what gifts they bring, and what baggage they bear. I've learned who could hurt me and who could save me, who to trust and who to steer clear of. Who could teach me and who could learn a thing or two from me. And second, all the folks who have come and gone, all the experiences I've had, all the jottings and drawings in those notebooks—these are thoughts on how to live as daring and creative a life as I can possibly live. And how better to affirm the holiness, the blessing of life, than to live it to the fullest?"

She stops here and sits back in her chair. A smile slowly stretches across her face, and her eyes brighten. "It starts, aptly enough, at the beginning."

For Cathrine, "the beginning" was Columbia, Missouri, just over six decades ago, where her father, a Methodist minister, served as a chaplain to the students at the state university. It was there, in the first years of her life, that she began to vaguely comprehend what she's taken a lifetime to fully appreciate: that the world could be a place of wonder and peril, that some people could be trusted to look out for her best interests and some people couldn't, and that even perilous situations could be adventurous—and educational—ones as well.

"So many students came and went in our home. Foreign students would teach me words in their native tongue. Others, some of whom I might never have met before, would take me out for 'discovery' walks, or otherwise look after me. I found them to be wonderful, and even if I didn't know where they were taking me, I always felt safe around them. That said, the one person I remember in particular was this guy, a student, who would never make eye contact with me. I must've been no more than five or six years old, a real innocent, and I remember thinking, 'I don't like this guy, because he won't look me in the eye.' It may have been a harsh judgment on my part—maybe he was just painfully shy—but one of the things that's always been important to me both then and since has been person-to-person contact, and even at that young age I was wary of someone who refused me that contact, refused to 'let me in.'"

It was her first mental notation for the little black box. "That story is metaphor for me," she tells me, "because to this day I want so much to connect with people, and not just people with whom I have things in common, people who I'm naturally drawn to. I also want—I've always wanted—to know how to connect with people I don't like or maybe I just don't 'get.' People whose politics or tastes or values or religion are different than mine. They challenge my judgments and stretch my imagination, and I like that. That's how I learn." Some of her jottings bear this out: "I don't know about this one," she writes of someone she's just met, "but I want to." And of another, "She has a heart of gold and a mind of stone; I hope we talk some more."

Over the years there has been a motley collection of hearts and minds with whom she's mixed and from whom she's learned. The lessons have not always come easily, and they have sometimes borne a great price, but to Cathrine's discerning eye, each encounter has made her a somehow richer, wiser, deeper human being. "People can't always be depended on," she writes in one entry, "but they can be depended on to make me think."

## EUROPEAN ADVENTURE

From this point on, Cathrine does not tell her story chronologically so much as episodically, each event another doodle or thought or scribble or sketch preserved somewhere in its appropriate cubby in the little black box, like marginalia that make sense out of random scribbles.

"There was the stretch of time in London," she begins; "I was hanging out with some real free thinkers and rubbing elbows with the likes of not-yet-famous creative types like Leonard Cohen, David Bowie, [the feminist writer] Lynne Tillman (and being awakened at least once by the eminently famous McCartney, a friend of a friend). We had a kind of artists' colony that we'd founded and housed in an old dilapidated warehouse. It was an avant-garde, 'anything goes' sort of place—theater, poetry, literary readings, films—a place where a lot of creative juices flowed, at least until the government stepped in and turned off the spigot. They considered some of the stuff we were doing to be a little too risqué, you see. They not only shut us down; they asked us non-Brits to leave the country." Like so many chapters in her life, Cathrine harbors no bitterness or regret.

"We didn't make a dime and would rather have stayed, but it was another one of those examples of, on the one hand, some wonderful souls sustaining me after a very rough time in my life, and on the other hand, some other folks who just seemed too intellectually sclerotic to get a handle on what we were about. I wouldn't have traded it for the world." As she would write years later in one of her notebooks, "A roller-coaster dark space in me spirals up and down through friends, careers, loops, dreams, visions. . . ."

From London the roller-coaster would make stops in Spain, Tangiers, Morocco, Amsterdam, and Toronto, each becoming another course in her global education.

"Let me tell you about this extraordinary thing that happened to me in Morocco," she says, leaning forward with characteristic enthusiasm. "It really enlightened me about what was then a very, very nascent global feminist movement.

"Back here in the States, Gloria Steinem and Betty Friedan had been interviewed for *Newsweek* about this new movement, and a lot of the article dealt with women's freedom to find self-expression. It was all about not being subject to male expectations, male desires, and all that sort of thing. Now, here I was in this very conservative country, very patriarchal, strict Muslim, with most of the women wearing burkas, so all I could ever see of them were their eyes. Not a lot of self-expression, or so I thought."

At this point I remind her of the young man in her Missouri days who would not make eye contact with her, and I ask her whether or not there was in fact some level of self-expression being offered up by these women revealed *only* in their eyes.

"Absolutely!" she beams. "What I came to discover was that these women were very, very expressive! Let me tell you what happened. One afternoon I went into one of these public baths, where the burkas came off and revealed these beautiful women with gorgeous makeup and perfume and jewelry and really stunning henna tattoos. And then it dawned on me how self-expressive these seemingly repressed women were, because it was all about expressing themselves *to one another*: expressing themselves in each other's company. So in one of the notebooks I have a little drawing of a woman in a burka that I found years later, as a reminder of this trip and this lesson."

I ask Cathrine if she has any writings or drawings from the trip itself, and she turns serious and sullen. "This really tears at me. I lost a lot of those notebooks, and I'll tell you why.

"A friend and I had been living on a tiny island off the coast of Spain, Ibiza, where we ran a modest restaurant. At one point we had to return to the United States for some business, but while we were gone [the fascist Spanish dictator Francisco] Franco decided he'd had it with all the expat hippies hanging out on Ibiza, and the next thing we hear, people are dying, disappearing, being thrown in jail. Suddenly, the 'Summer of Love' was over, and it was time to leave. So all my journals of those years were lost to Ibiza, which just crushes me."

"It's not important how we came together, but I met this artist, this bigger-than-life man with the heart of a poet and the body of a linebacker. His name was Gordon Raynor. It wasn't a romantic relationship—he had a girlfriend, and they were very tight. Gordon was a real 'alpha' guy, with a big handlebar mustache, a great bellowing voice that was just a little too loud for the rest of the room, and a coterie of followers who, at his insistence, took me in as one of their own. I was, of course, broke and effectively homeless. I often say that if not for him, I might not have survived a brutal Canadian winter, might not have appreciated how important it is to have a mentor, and might not have learned how to drink Southern Comfort in one gulp—all lessons that have served me well over the years." A winsome look comes across her

face as with obvious fondness she remembers this kind wonderful man who was a very brief part of her life nearly forty
years ago.

She rifles through one of the notebooks and shows me a
more or less expressionistic painting he had done and given to
her. A kind of Jackson Pollock meets Maxfield Parrish composition, it is a riot of swirls and colors jumping off the page
in dizzying, head-spinning movement, at once charming in its
simplicity and overwhelming in its intensity. It strikes me that
Gordon may have given Cathrine this *particular* piece of work
because it so accurately captures his barely contained chaos
that, a generation later, still brings her warm feelings and vivid
memories.

## TO OZ

Eventually Cathrine realized a fantasy she first nurtured when
she was a young girl sitting in her mother's lap and looking
at the cartoons in *The New Yorker* magazine. Having traveled
internationally for a good many years, she now sought anchor-
age in the most international of cities, so in the early 1970s she
moved to the New York she had long dreamed about calling
her home, and it did not disappoint her. She settled in but
not down. Life became more routine but no less interesting
as she pitched her tent in the hip downtown neighborhood of
Chelsea, immersed herself in the city's culture, and marveled
at its sheer audacity. She continued to write, not only in her
journals but professionally as well.

Over the ensuing years Cathrine authored books, screenplays, documentaries, and educational guides. She joined
book clubs and became a driving force in an informal "church
without walls," which was, in effect, a fellowship of believers
immersed in their faith journeys but unburdened by what they
believed to be crusted doctrines or rigid dogmas. She gloried

in the city's incomparable arts scene and collection of intelligentsia, but equally relished its gritty, *noir* underbelly and the idiosyncratic population that lived there. She married a wonderful man with whom she raised two feisty, fiercely independent, yet deeply devoted daughters.

In one of the entries, in one of the journals, in a year now long past, Cathrine has made a pen-and-ink drawing of a room in her first New York apartment. Plants stand in the corner of the sparsely furnished but brightly sunlit room, and a cat sits peering out the lone window. The sketch exudes a certain serenity, fleshed out by the script that accompanies it: "I'm happy," Cathrine has written, "because I don't have to understand everything. And I'm almost sane and my cat isn't." She is finding peace in the world, but for her, peace must necessarily include just a steady-enough diet of latent, leavening New York lunacy, if only to keep things interesting.

## TWILIGHT

It is late in the afternoon, and we have been talking for several hours now. We are alone, and it is quiet as we sit in the shadows. She is looking with affection at her little black box, absentmindedly running her hand along one of its edges, and fiddling with the lock on her "stash compartment." She cocks her head slightly, pauses for a moment, and makes something of a confession.

"The pot," she begins, and then pauses. "It really does help me think creatively. But now it also helps counter some of the effects of the chemo."

Cathrine's life has again been stirred by opposing forces, one camp hostile to her and the other protective of her. As always, there is much to be learned:

"I've had three bouts of cancer over the past three and a half years. The first go-round, I thought it pretty troublesome but beatable. When it came back a second time, I said to myself, 'Okay, there's some lesson here, and I'm not getting it. I'm getting the cancer, but I'm not getting the lesson.' I say this because I've always felt that this is how we redeem tragedy and difficulty in our life. We find some utility in it.

"Only of late has it dawned on me that as much as I've had God's angels shepherd me through some very tough times, there's always been a part of me that wanted to see myself as self-reliant. So while on one hand I've welcomed their generosity, on the other I've kept them at bay.

"I've been seeing a psychotherapist who specializes in treating people with cancer. Her name is Barbara, and she's a very wise and deeply spiritual woman, who's helped me understand that I haven't fully trusted people to love me without feeling as though I need to repay them. But now I pretty much have to: I have to accept their love without paying it back, and it's been unspeakably wonderful. The calls, the notes, the food, the visits—I'm receiving it all now, and I don't feel like I owe anyone anything in return. I'm allowing those who love me to do just that. I'm overwhelmed." I remind her of a phrase I once used in a sermon, to the effect that sometimes, when we are in pain, a bad theology is no match for a good casserole. She nods in agreement.

The third incursion has led Cathrine to accept that her time is significantly more limited than it would've been had she not contracted this disease. "It's stage-four colon cancer. I don't think I'm gonna beat it," she tells me with typical matter-of-factness. "God knows I'm gonna try, but I have my doubts. Which is why the black box is even more important to me now than ever before. It's a good time to look back on a life well lived, and to add whatever remains to be added."

In deference to the age in which we live, and perhaps as a paean to her father's late-life career as a filmmaker, Cathrine's latest addition is not in a journal or notebook but in a brief video she produced and posted on the Internet. In thinking about her life with cancer, she uses the occasion to tell us:

"As a child *of* the '60s, my adventures, my lovers are all bigger than life. As a child *in* my 60s, death will come sooner not later, and when it comes, I will have consumed every second, blessed most days, cursed a couple. . . . Cancer will end my life, but it won't define it. I am not my disease, neither victim nor survivor. I am simply Cathrine, *and I am living my life like there's no tomorrow.*"

Indeed she is. As a child in her 60s who never finished high school, who counts each day as precious and has serious doubts about how many more are in the ledger, Cathrine is preparing to return to college, but this time as a student. Shortly after our last conversation, she was accepted into a writing program. At Bennington College. She found her grail, living, as she always has, like there's no tomorrow.

Cathrine's stories offer us a contemporary spin on an ancient story; she is the modern Moses, an exodus wanderer who embraced her travel as eagerly as she sought her destination. She not only sought her Canaan, her land of milk and honey; she also remained ever attuned to the hints of grace she found along the way. As though manna was, if not falling from heaven, then hidden at every turn, Cathrine had an uncanny ability to find the wondrous, the godlike, the gold amid the dross. As her old friend Leonard Cohen put it in one of his ballads, "She shows you where to look among the garbage and the flowers." From a Los Angeles tenement to a London theatre to an Ibiza café to a Moroccan bathhouse to an iconoclastic church community in bohemian New York City, challenges became revelations, obstacles became opportunities, strangers became lifelines, and in some instances, lifelong friends.

I believe each place was redolent with meaning because Cathrine held on to one singular article of faith that either sustained her in this journey or anchored her in whatever place that journey happened to land her. Cathrine was a woman with the courage to embrace Christ's entreaty to have faith in things unseen. "Do not worry about your life, what you will eat or what you will drink, or about your body, what you will wear. Is not life more than food and the body more than clothing?" he asked his followers (Matt. 6:25 NRSV). And so it was for her, much, much more than food and clothing.

Poverty was a frequent companion. Destitution hung like a Damoclean sword above the many festivities that were her life. World events impinged on her Aquarian efforts to live in harmony with the universe. People she wanted to trust proved untrustworthy. And yet she always managed to find the flowers in the garbage.

A more cautious person might have played things much safer, much closer to the vest, and such a person could be forgiven for doing so if it meant sparing themselves the anxieties attendant in wondering where her next meal was going to come from or whether the kindness a stranger extended to her on one day would be revoked the next. But that person also would have been denied so many of the kinds of adventures that helped define a life as having been blessed in substance if not in length. In final analysis it was by faith—in God, in herself, in the beneficence of others—that Cathrine propelled herself from one extraordinary moment to the next, always open to the lessons that that moment was ready to yield. She not only found her Canaan; she found so many little Canaans along the way. And unlike the protagonists of the ancient story, her faith never wavered.

Cathrine Kellison was the high school dropout with the world-class education, the lily of the field spun and grown and made beautiful by the grace of God. Cathrine's life was testimony to the power that life holds when we live it with greater faith in things we cannot see than concern for things we can see.

*Postscript:* Two weeks before the start of the term at Bennington, Cathrine died. There's no tomorrow. There also were no regrets.

## Questions for Discussion

1. Talk about the discipline of journaling as a part of an examined life.
2. Reflect on the story Cathrine tells of being in the Moroccan baths with the native women. How is prejudice (literally, "prejudgment") the product of too little information? Have there been times in your life when you have made a hasty judgment only to have it disabused later?
3. Cathrine lived much of her life with faith in things unseen, a high-wire act with no net. Is this something you see yourself capable of? If not, is it something you envy in others? Would your life be richer with more risk?

# Survivors

Chapter 11

# JANE PAULEY
## Through the Glass Faintly

*I love the light . . . but not the glare.*
—Jane Pauley

## THE LIGHT OF THE WORLD

It is one of those crisp and clear pre-spring days that augurs more warmth than it delivers but reminds you that, while you are standing between a season of darkness and a season of light, your feet are pointed in the direction you want to be going. Easter is drawing near as Christmas's chill fades to memory, and frozen ground yields to the dogged crocus elbowing its way upward. I enter veteran journalist Jane Pauley's New York City apartment, and she offers me a seat in the living room, modest of size by some standards but high ceilinged and gracefully decorated in calm, natural tones of tan and light green. At this early hour the room is illuminated by the soft glow of morning sun coming to us through a wall of glass that looks east, the natural light diffused by a translucent white curtain hanging floor to ceiling. On the other side of the curtain is a garden, beyond which there is a wall, and then the

East River. We settle into a corner, facing in the direction of the light, she on the sofa and me in an easy chair. Modestly elegant, exceedingly comfortable.

From where she sits, Jane begins to explain to me the importance of the space for her, the focal point of which is the curtain of diffused sunlight, and as she does so, it slowly dawns on me that what she is describing may well be the thing she most cherishes: her portal to the divine.

"This place, at this time of day, with me sitting in this corner, sunlight being filtered in and illuminating the room so softly, . . . this is my calm space, where I feel safe, and secure, and where I am wanting for absolutely nothing."

I ask her what it is about *this* time of day that makes the room so special, and she answers, "It's not just the light. It's also the shadows." In other words, she goes on, it's not just where the light goes; it's also where it doesn't go. "I love light, but I think of it like a flow of energy; too much of it, and I feel bombarded. Too little, and I'm in the dark. I need the spigot turned on just so, and that's what I feel when I see the light coming to me through the curtain."

She continues with her thoughts. "Apropos of your book, a fire can warm a house or burn it down, just as water can quench a thirst or drown a person. When I look at the curtain, I see it as a metaphor, letting certain things into my life but in moderation, a little muted, controlled. Not overwhelming me. She studies the curtain for a moment and then points out the silhouettes of a number of objects—tree branches, clay pots, a slatted wooden bench, a short wall—on the other side of the glass, objects whose shadows work together to create their own monochromatic artistic montage. She points out two in particular:

"I look at the gray outline of the willow branches [in the right-hand corner]. I see them stirring gently with the breeze, and I notice the buds that are soon to break and flower. It recalls to my mind the Hindu concept of the tree of life, eternal rejuvenation. But then beyond the branches I also see the silhouette of a thin thread of barbed wire that somebody [a previous owner] strung across the top of the wall that separates our garden from the river, and that's suggestive to me of the risks in life, which are no less real than the beauties. So here is this vivid contrast between comfort and challenge, and I find myself drawn to it. I realize that what's really important for me is not the objects per se, but how they come to me; it's the filtered light that's really important. Neither the branches nor the wire are inherently good or inherently bad: they just simply *are*. They're simply a part of existence, just like comfort and challenge." Nudged a bit, she expands on this:

"If the willow branch conjures up images of comfort, it also reminds me that in my desire to find comfort, quiet, and serenity, I can go overboard; I can cut out a whole lot of external stimuli and drift into a state of isolation."

From here Jane went on to talk about how this dichotomy between challenge and comfort has been born out in her struggles with bipolar disorder, first brought on back in 2001 by medication she had been given for the treatment of hives, and for which she was treated, as an in-patient at a psychiatric hospital, for about three weeks later that year.

"When you're prone to depression, isolation is not only an easy place to float off to," she tells me; "it can also deepen and prolong the depression. With that in mind, not only am I extremely faithful about taking my medications; I'm also on constant lookout for 'triggers' that can induce my depression. When I sense it coming on, one of the things I try to do is get out of that seductive comfort zone, do things I don't necessarily feel the desire to do but things—like socializing or traveling or writing a speech or delivering that speech—that I know to be good for me. You might say I force myself to take my eyes off the willow branches and look at the barbed wire."

I ask her what specifically comes to mind when, in this context, she contemplates that barbed wire. She thinks for a minute, stares out through the curtain, then answers.

"Let me tell you a little story. I was in a hair salon one afternoon, *really* getting pampered: hair, nails, comfort to the max. Very pleasurable. Even indulgent. My eye catches a quote in a magazine I'm reading. It's [the actress] Jennifer Aniston commenting on how almost everything you most want in life lies *just beyond* your comfort zone.

"Her sentiment stayed with me because I think of myself as someone who, for whatever success I've enjoyed in life, has found that success when I've pushed myself beyond my comfort zone, taken on the barbed wire. In fact, I don't think of myself as someone who succeeds at all she does, but I do think of myself as someone who always tries.

"Not long ago I gave a speech that I titled 'Trying Times,' with the title being a double entendre. We are living through trying times, but that also makes them good times to be *trying*, to be trying new things, and that was my point. It takes some courage and perseverance to try new things, to go beyond our comfort zones, and I like to think that both in my career and in my battle with this illness, I've shown some of both. I aspire to be someone who tries, who does things that do not come easily for me and therefore carry a sense of risk.

"My years at the *Today* show were like this, especially when we were on location. I've always felt best at home, with my family around me. 'Stay-at-Home Jane' is much stronger than 'Adventure Jane.' So when we would go to these far-flung places around the world—China, Monaco, the Vatican, Korea—as exotic as it might have seemed to the television audience, it was hard for me. I wanted to be home. But by trying, by facing the challenge, I found that I could rise to the occasion and do what I had to do. In the end, I think these kinds of experiences are good for me. They force me to maintain the balance. They also made the return to my comfort zone more acceptable to me.

"Now, when I give addresses like the 'Trying Times' speech, this is one of the things I want to impart to my audience. To find that balance of energy, between comfort and daring, satisfaction and risk, calm and challenge."

With this observation, Jane rests her index finger on her cheek, slightly knits her brow, and does a visual sweep of the room, as though she is drawing deep upon the sense of peace it is giving her while also being keenly aware of the fact that, at least for the moment, she is not letting it take her to a place of extremes. The filter is working. She begins to point out other objects in the room—an Audubon rendering of a baying wolf and another of a wolverine, both suggestive of aggression but offset by a Mokara orchid on the coffee table and a Japanese print that hangs above where I am sitting—that carry this theme of translucence for her, the sense that life can be seen as being comprised of proper doses of light and shadow, safety and risk.

"I think I've been a disappointment to you," she then confesses, self-deprecatingly. "You're looking for some great theological insight, and I just don't have one!" I couldn't disagree more, of course. In fact, I found great spiritual wisdom in what she had to say, much of which fittingly comes through to me as filtered, as if through a veil of understanding.

## REVELATION

I do not believe God comes to us in a thunderbolt as much as in hint, wisp, or whisper, what the great medieval philosopher Maimonides called "a spiritual perception" unlike anything we perceive with our senses. When we study Scripture or muse on the complexity of the universe, the subtlety of God's presence is slowly made known to us. When we grieve over inexplicable loss or revel in the gift of unbidden grace, God's infinite, immeasurable, indecipherable love is transmuted to us through very human means and in very human terms. Revelation is not so much God in our midst as it is God in metaphor, the ineffable delivered to us in tangible terms. Thus when we say we experience God's mercy, for instance, what we are really saying is that the experience of incomprehensible mercy has come to us in terms that we can comprehend. We put words on something that lies beyond words and in so doing rely on the language of approximation because our usual language does not depict the nature of God so much as it points to something that cannot be communicated by human argot: the spiritual perception.

This is why at Sinai, God comes to Moses "in a thick cloud, that the people may hear when I speak with you" (Exod. 19:9); and why later in the story, God tells Moses, "You cannot see my face; for no one shall see me and live" (33:20 NRSV). It is why in the story of the transfiguration of Jesus, the disciples who witness it are depicted as having fallen "face down, filled with awe" (Matt. 17:6, my trans.), because without "a thick cloud" to mediate their experience, their senses were overwhelmed; they could not fully take in what they were witnessing. And finally, what, after all, was Christ for Christians if not a mediator between human and divine?

I think of revelation as coming to us to us not through the harsh glare of a blinding light but diffused, as if by Jane's translucent curtain, where the truth is evident without being overpowering, bespeaking something larger than itself without obscuring itself by virtue of its mere grandeur in the face of our modest stature. I think of this when I consider Jane's observation about the morning sunlight coming in from the east but being buffered by the curtain in her living room, and how for her it is symbolic of her need to receive what life has to give her in measured manner. She doesn't want to live in the darkness of isolation, but neither does she want, in her words, "to be bombarded" with life's incessant input—even when that input is the sort of thing that comforts her and gives her joy—in a magnitude that can be too much for her to handle. Her curtain, then, is her "thick cloud." It is that which allows her to hear life speak to her and not be deafened by it.

## REVELATION, BUT FOR WHAT PURPOSE?

When Jane seized upon the shadowed images of the budding willow and the barbed wire, she interpreted them as symbolizing, among other things, comfort and challenge; and here too she was (perhaps unconsciously) striking a theological chord. For if God is revealed to us through the shroud of existence, then to what end and for what purpose if not to both comfort us in our challenges and challenge us in our comforts? If we are truly receptive to God, we are becalmed by the words that come to us in our hymns, our prayers, our readings, and our meditations, whose purpose is to strengthen us when our spirits flag and bolster us when our doubts persist. When we read of David being assured that the Lord is his shepherd, we know that the Lord is ours as well; just as when Jesus told the gathered masses that "those who mourn . . . will be comforted" (Matt. 5:4 NRSV), we know that this includes all people at all times in all manners of distress. When we hear the rousing words of the old African American spiritual that "there is a balm in Gilead . . . to heal the sin-sick soul," we know, too, that God is not indifferent to our sufferings or the sufferings of our people and will find ways, however overt or sublime, to soothe and succor them.

But as much as we may find refuge in these, our "willow-bud moments," we cannot live in refuge any more than Jane can live in the splendid isolation of her sybaritic little comfort zone. Consider the resurrection story as it's recounted in Matthew 28: When Mary Magdalene and "the other" Mary arrive at the tomb, they're astonished, thrilled, "filled with joy," according to the author, to find that it's empty. With this last great earthly gesture, Jesus has shown that divine love conquers all, even death. If ever there was a more comforting balm to soothe the sin-sick souls of the anxious, I can't imagine what it is. If only the story ended there.

It doesn't. As the women are hastening to tell the disciples what they've seen, they encounter the risen Christ, who instructs them, "Tell my brothers to go to Galilee. . . ."

Go to Galilee! In other words, do not remain where it is comfortable and safe simply *because* it is comfortable and safe, but go to unknown places where challenges wait to question your mettle and test your faith. Don't become absorbed in the promise of the heavenly resurrection at the expense of the earthly mission, where so much remains undone. Go to Galilee, where you can dare to challenge the assumptions that have kept you from realizing your potential as a human being. Go to where you can take the risks of love and loss, where to be fully alive means to scale the walls that separate your fears from your courage, where involvement trumps isolation, where your talents are tested and failure to accomplish is of greater worth than failure to act. Go to Galilee, where you will find hungry children who must be fed with more than the promise that better days are ahead. Go to the Galilee of the inconsolable widow, the wounded veteran, the mentally ill, for whom a word of encouragement from someone they admire and respect can mean more to them than all the medication they've thus far received.

Go to the Galilee of your heart, your hope, your fear, your challenge, your discomfort. It is waiting for you just on the other side of the barbed-wire wall. Scale that wall; you may even find some budding branches on the other side.

# SANCTUARY

Finally, I found a church-like quality to this setting that Jane was holding in such high esteem, not just because of the safety offered by a sun-soaked living room sanctuary, but also because of the greater expanses that it calls us to. In early American New England, the pilgrims built their churches in the center of town, not on its fringes, and installed clear glass panes, not stained-glass windows. There was a reason for this. As church historian James Dittes once explained to me, "They never wanted anyone who was in worship to lose sight of the outside world, so at Sunday worship all the parishioners needed to be able to look *out* those windows and see the church as directly ensconced in the very heart of things.

"But the reverse was true as well," Dittes continued. "They also wanted the unchurched, the ones outside the sanctuary walls, to be able to look *in* those windows, where the very real and very rewarding work of worship was bringing great meaning to the lives of the congregants, and where they could feel invited by people who had nothing to hide, rather than being separated by the opacity of a wooden wall or a stained-glass window. They wanted the work of the church to be transparent to the needs of the world."

And so it may be for Jane, whose history is one in which she has experienced on the one hand great success and greater happiness, and on the other hand the extraordinary challenges posed by the demons of her illness and her uncertainties. When she looks inward, may she find the peace of a God whose love holds and bears and tends and spares her. And when she looks outward, may she find a God whose same love compels and encourages and beckons and believes in her. Indeed, may it be for all of us.

## Questions for Discussion

1. Jane speaks a good deal about the need for moderation in her life. What are the things that overwhelm you from time to time? How can you counteract them?

2. One in twenty people over the age of twelve experience some form of clinical depression at some point in their lives. What do you suppose (or know) to be some of the most common misconceptions about depression?

3. Discuss the idea of revelation, not only from the standpoint of theology but also from the standpoint of everyday life. How, for instance, are truths or lies revealed to us? How are we best disposed to receive revelations? What do we do to shut them out? Why do we need "screens" the way Jane does?

# Chapter 12

# DON LANGE

## *The Wounded Warrior*

*I got there too late. The house burned down seven years ago.*
—Don Lange

IF THE HEADLINES IN THAT DAY'S *NEW YORK TIMES* ARE ANY INDICA-
tion, March 30, 2003, was by all accounts another unremarkable Sunday, with a sizeable chunk of the paper's attention
lavished on whether a late-season snow squall was going to
delay the next day's opening of the major league baseball season. (Unfortunately for us New Yorkers, it didn't; the lamen-
table Mets were throttled by the Cubs 15–2 on their way to yet
another last place finish.) And if the notes in my own calendar
are any indication, the day was a similar yawner for me. A
little Syracuse basketball on TV, dinner and a movie with my
wife and daughter, and a few notes written for a book I was
working on at the time, some insipid thoughts that seemed
inspired at the time but mercifully found their proper home in
the jaws of the paper shredder.

Halfway around the world was a different scene entirely.
Deep in the godforsaken terrain of a country most Americans
couldn't have found on a map two years earlier, there was no

such luxury of lassitude for Don Lange. Lange, a thirty-six-year-old Virginia native and Marine Gunnery Sergeant found himself frontline in a war that few of us back in the States wanted to fight and most of us would just as soon either forget about or make believe never happened. Instead of being with his wife and daughter that day, heading to the movies or the mall, he was with his unit, heading into battle. Yes, they were concerned about the weather, but not as it pertained to baseball. Their anxiety was over whether a desert sandstorm, so common that time of year in and around Afghanistan, might impede their mission. What happened to Don on March 30 is difficult to piece together, in part because he's not at liberty to divulge the particulars of that mission and in part because he had his brain jarred with such crushing force and blinding intensity that for him, seven years out, the day remains more rumor than recollection.

Memory loss. It's just one of the tricks the brain will play on you when it is subjected to repeated shock waves in excess of a thousand pounds per square inch, courtesy of successive rocket-propelled grenades (commonly known as RPGs; one of so many acronyms that have found their way into our lexicon since the outbreak of this war) launched at his convoy by the Taliban or their surrogates. But it is not the only trick. In fact, there are so many permutations of traumatic brain injury (TBI, yet another) that doctors and researchers are no longer shocked by effects that might to the untrained eye seem novel or bizarre. Given the complexity of the human brain, with trillions of synaptic connections that fire up between its billions of cells, what scientists know about its capacity for injury and rehabilitation could, in the words of one prominent brain surgeon, "fit in a thimble and still leave room for a small thumb."

In Don's case there was a goodly amount of wreckage, not only between the ears but also below the neck, so recuperation

in the weeks and months that followed included long, sometimes grueling hours of speech therapy, occupational therapy,
physical therapy, and psychotherapy (not to mention waves of
loneliness and boredom interspersed with indulgences of well-
warranted self-pity). Rehab was more than a full-time job; it
was a way of life. In addition to suffering impaired executive
functioning, he was diagnosed with post-injury attention def-
icit disorder (ADD). Not surprisingly, fits of depression set
in, sometimes acute and sometimes protracted, sometimes
induced neurologically and sometimes precipitated by his
environment. Seven years later it still comes and goes; he is
still being treated with drugs, and for a long stretch of time he
was also treated for posttraumatic stress disorder (PTSD, yet
*another* neologism). A sometimes unforgiving affective condition that can sneak up and catch the sufferer unawares, PTSD
is often characterized by flashbacks, night trauma, hypersen-
sitivity to imagined threats, and rapid and seemingly arbitrary
mood swings. The perniciousness of PTSD is only com-
pounded by its insidiousness: it is invisible to the untutored
eye and therefore frequently dismissed by others (including, as
often as not, military personnel) as little more than weakness
of will on the part of the one who is suffering from it. "Suck
it up," the soldier is told, even when he feels as if he's been
sucked dry.

There's more. Probably as a result of the injury on the
frontal lobe of his brain, when Don speaks, it is often slowly
and with great deliberation; he appears less to be choosing
his sentences than rummaging through a disorganized bin full
of random words and phrases, as though he is trying to get
his hands on the ones that best convey what it is he wants to
communicate. ("Where's that noun I was looking for? I know
it was here a minute ago. . . .") As we speak, I find myself
waiting longer than usual for responses to my questions, and
forcing myself to take longer pauses before I pose a follow-up

query. I make sure Don has finished his thoughts and is ready to move on rather than simply caught up in what feels to me like an inordinately long pause, as if he's snagged himself on an errant non sequitur, a burr in the brush that he didn't see lying there. Eventually I become accustomed to this rhythm rather than forcing patience upon myself; as I do, I come to realize that Don has quietly trained me to work at his pace rather than my leaning into him to work at mine. I suspect he does a lot of this. Adaptive behaviors can sometimes entail getting the other person to adapt.

There are other random incarnations of his condition as well, some more annoyances than disabilities. A normal hum of ambient noise in a restaurant or public plaza can make a poetry reading sound like a Metallica concert on steroids. It can become difficult if not impossible for Don to hear a conversation that is being directed to him by someone just a foot or two away. On occasion he detects smells that don't exist, phantom smells, no doubt because the olfactory nerve, which runs from the back of the nasal passages right through center of brain, endured significant trauma in the assault. He is also saddled with what he calls cognitive fatigue, a limit on just how much content his brain can process during the course of a day before, as he puts it, his "batteries run dry." Switching metaphors, he tells me that "it's like having a limited amount of cash in the bank each day, and when it runs out, it runs out. If I'm out in the afternoon, and there's no 'money in the till,' I might forget where I live. I'll wind up sitting on a park bench until two or three in the morning, when a cop might come along and get me home."

All this notwithstanding, although it takes a little more work for him to gather his thoughts and then express them in a cogent manner, if you spend just ten minutes with Don, you can't help but be impressed by how insightful, thoughtful, and perceptive a man he is. He is also Marine-handsome, tallish, with chiseled good looks, Uncle Sam eyes, close-cropped hair, and a physique that suggests someone much younger than his forty-plus years. On top of this, he manages to have a wry, understated sense of humor, no doubt a useful asset throughout the more rigorous stretches of his recovery.

Though I don't mention it to him, I notice that Don also prefers to sit with his back to a wall, particularly in public places, and I wonder if this is perhaps a lingering vestige of the hypervigilance that comes with PTSD. If so, it represents just one more in a litany of other adaptive behaviors Don has been forced to assume as he has learned to disengage from his old self in order to embrace a new reality. It is also one reminder of how his journey since that day in March of 2003 is emblematic of the tens of thousands of wounded veterans whose backs are against the wall, whose life paths have taken severe and imposed detours, just as my journey over that same span of time is emblematic of a nation they served that continued to shuffle along more or less unaffected to the point of being uninterested. So Don and the Dons of this country will wonder if he can make it home before his brain decides to call it quits for the day while I and millions like me are wondering if the baseball season will start on time or what's playing at the local movie house.

## A NEW BEING

Regarding the day of the attack, Don tells me in a rather deadpan fashion that *perhaps* the most dramatic thing that happened to him as a result of his injury is that he died. Picking up on his sardonic tone, I parry back that, yeah, I suppose I can see how that might be construed by some people as kind of a big deal. He smiles and waits patiently for the inevitable follow-up question. We are doing a little pas de deux—with him holding the upper hand—that he has clearly danced before, and so I obligingly take the bait and ask for him to expand on this.

"So, Don, you say that you died. Exactly how'd you pull that off?" He then gets very serious with me; he wants to be absolutely clear in what he says and how I hear it.

"While I have intact memories of my life before the injury, memories of things, events, actions, feelings, I feel disconnected from them. I cannot recall what I was thinking or feeling in the midst of these events. I recall them, but I don't recall how I *interpreted* them, what they *meant* to me, or how they felt from the inside out." Then he uses this helpful analogy: "Imagine seeing an actor in a play and trying to interpret that actor's thoughts and feelings. You are not the actor, and you don't feel like the actor. You merely *observe* the actor." In other words, Don Lange finds himself a passive observer to a performance that is his own past, his own life story, sitting alone in the empty theater, an audience of one: *Don Lange, this is your life! It just so happens you don't remember living it.*

"And this is why there's nothing for me to rescue from your burning building," he confides with a calm that belies the enormity of what he is saying. "I arrived too late. The timbers were just still smoldering. Everything was already gone. *I was gone.*" *I was gone.* This phrase, hanging large in the silence between us like a storm cloud at a company picnic, is why he strove for such crystal clarity. Breaking that silence, he goes on to offer another example, as if to amplify his point:

"When I am asked, 'Why did you join the Marines?' I can only go by what my father has later told me, that it was an act of rebellion. Now, I can recall other instances of rebellion that seem consistent with this, so I believe it to be true. In other words, I remember the *what* but not the *why*." He continues to speak, Vulcan-like, with the analytical distance of one who is interpreting a passage from a story in a book that is either someone else's autobiography or raw fiction. He adds: "Now,

I carried over many of the same likes and dislikes, . . . but my 'resurrected' version has a completely different way of thinking, with different and more carefully defined beliefs."

I ask him to explain how he thinks differently now, and he begins his reply with a caveat that again reminds me (as if I needed reminding) of his "death": "I can answer your question, but I have to make some assumptions here, because I can't recall how I used to think." That said, he continues, "I seem to be conducting my life differently now than I did before the injury.'" He cites two points in particular.

"To begin with, I surround myself with different people than I used to. The people in my inner circle are a very compassionate lot, and this is new for me." Don then goes on to offer an observation that has me wondering if this is a function of the people around him or of his own disposition: "I didn't used to have an inner circle," he tells me. "It was a wider circumference but with a thinly populated core, with fewer intimate friends." It's a wonderful illustration, suggesting as it does that with him at the core, the wider the circumference, the farther away he is from the people. In his new life, what he lost in number he gained in intimacy.

Whatever its genesis, the quality of these new friendships is a product of a new disposition; Don is either disposed to, in his words, allowing more compassionate people to be close to him, or he is disposed to allowing that part of himself to surface that invites shared compassion with others. Yet the end result is the same: a greater sense of mutual vulnerability than he might have enjoyed in his previous life among people who love and trust one another.

A second major change he has made is something of a more intricate matter. Since he was brought up in the Roman Catholic Church and was no more or less obedient to the church than any self-identified rebel, Don has of late come to explore his faith in ways that have both deepened it and cut it loose from its old orthodoxy. He explains it this way: "In my 'previous life' I would ask, 'Why am I here?' and would answer it (or so I recall) by saying, 'I'm here to learn about myself, to learn about God, and to learn about the relationship I have with God.'" The lifelessness in his voice betrays a lack of conviction about this answer, a boilerplate, one-size-fits-all cliché that now feels to him like the religious equivalent of overcooked vegetables: vague, bland, largely inoffensive, but only nominally nourishing.

But eager to explore the question with a little more brio, the postinjury Don not only began to immerse himself in a study of the doctrines of the church; he also expanded his inquiry to include a wide range of religious and philosophical disciplines, eventually zeroing in on certain aspects of Zen Buddhism and the Stoicism of the Greek philosopher Zeno and the Roman thinker Seneca. From this amalgam of sources, he distilled one overriding and decidedly *un*orthodox principle:

"I'm much more precise now in understanding why I'm here," he explains. "I am here to develop the character that I will take with me in my immortal life beyond this physical universe." Here he comes to life, delivering this dictum with the enthusiasm of a man who has spent long hours trying to decode an exceedingly complex, maddeningly elusive equation; its answer, once he arrives at it, is to his mind's eye both beyond clear and above refute. He has distilled life's most bewildering question to produce one seductively simple—if unorthodox—answer. It is not for me to say whether it is "true" or not; but for Don, it is true, it is Truth. In the vernacular of the church, it is his credo.

Though I'm tempted to ask Don to expand on his ideas of the afterlife, I am even more intrigued by what all of this means to the man who is living *this* life, who almost lost this life in battle at a young age. So I instead ask him to explain what he believes to be at the foundation of human character. He answers me in one word: "Choices."

I am struck not only by the succinctness of his answer but also by what it omits. If I have it straight, in Don's cosmological progression, the choices we make define the character we become, which we in turn carry with us in some tangible way into an intangible, eternal afterlife. His thinking not only puts a heavy burden and high stakes on human volition; it also by inference diminishes the role of external factors such as the family we are born into, the health we enjoy, or the arbitrariness of, say, one soldier's suffering severe injury on the field of battle while another emerges unscathed and a third avoids deployment altogether. I can't help but wonder if his emphasis on the power of choice is something of a counterbalance for having had his life so thoroughly disrupted by an event he was powerless to control and whose consequences he had no choice but to accept. While I puzzle over this, he gives me a hint as to why choice is so salvific for him. It goes back to an incident that might be considered something of a resurrection event. New life.

"It's about a year and a half after the injury, and I am in rehab," he begins. "I'm working with my speech pathologist and, frankly, whining to her about not being able to remember certain thought processes prior to TBI. As I've told you, this made it impossible for me to define who I was. The old me was dead." The therapist's gift was to take Don's predicament and invite him to not just come to terms with it but also to use it to his advantage.

"Maybe this is an opportunity for you to redefine yourself, any way you want," she tells him. To put it another way, she was daring him to shift his focus from who he no longer was to who he would like to be. From something lost that he was incapable of re-creating (and incapable of avoiding) to a new creation of his design. A tabula rasa, a clean slate. Rebirth. As he recounts this moment, with eyes wide and animated, with the eagerness of the apostle Paul on the road to Damascus, the words of e. e. cummings float through my own mind: "I who have died am alive again today. . . . this is the birth day of life and love . . . ."

It was this epiphany that threw Don into, in his words, his "first real serious study of Catholic doctrine," ultimately incorporating the other, non-Christian isms into his own unique theology, a theology that places immortality at the heart of faith, character at the heart of immortality, and choice at the heart of character.

With this as his backdrop, Don is quick to inventory the substance of some of the more momentous character-shaping choices he has made in erecting his "new" life, foremost among them being, in his words, "the need to let go of my old self." As he went about the business of putting the speech therapist's suggestion into play, he found himself stuck in a kind of temporal netherworld, past on one side, future on the other, but no footing in the present. He was like the cartoon coyote caught between the cliff he just ran off of and the one he hasn't yet reached, precariously suspended in midair. "I came to realize that I had to let go of my old, preattack identity," he told me, "but that meant mourning the death of that self, relegating it forever to memory, and giving up on the idea that he/I would ever return. It also meant I didn't yet have a full understanding of who I wanted to be."

Not a smooth and seamless process, his new life came in fits and starts. Punctuated by stretches of grief and sadness, the threat of immobilizing depression lurked in the background and, in the early going, would leap out in front of him, brazen, like a roadside sniper, unannounced, unanticipated, unwelcome, and meaning only to do harm. But as time has provided distance from the old, it has also crystallized the new.

In amplifying the new, Don goes on to point out other qualities he has assumed, other choices he has made, that help define the content of his character. He notes three in particular: "As I mentioned earlier, my friendships are deeper and more intimate, and that is most certainly by choice." To this he adds, "One of the things that has helped me sustain those relationships is a new and more useful understanding of blame. I now see that it is a largely unproductive partner to have. If my previous life hit a pothole, I would always be quick to hold someone accountable, but I've come to realize that no value is added to my life by blaming others for whatever might go wrong. I try very hard to be less prone to judgment." His new-found awareness is reminiscent of an old formula in marriage counseling, that when a disagreement arises, a couple has two choices: they can either fix the blame or fix the problem. Don has slid from the former to the latter. And finally, not unrelated to his emancipation from the need to find fault and lay blame, he mentions that he now holds "the firm conviction that in everything lousy that happens, there can be found the seed of something that can be beneficial to us in the future. Whether we choose to take advantage of it is up to us."

Whether indeed. Ultimately for Don, it is all about choice. When he says choice is what fashions the character that he will one day take with him to what the hymnist Albert Brumley has called "God's celestial shores," he is by logical extension defining it as the seminal component of his belief system. He *chooses* to enter into loving relationships. He *chooses* to forgo blame in favor of grace. He *chooses* to redeem the horror of his "death" by transforming himself into a new being. It is no surprise, I suspect, that a man who had no say in what befell him on the battlefield and all of its attendant consequences should come to revere the idea (and utility) of human volition as fundamental to his faith. He could have either been sunk by the curse of his circumstances or saved by the content of his choices. Don chose salvation over despair, and by doing so he echoed the words of the Deuteronomist when he wrote of God's admonition to the Hebrews: "I have set before you life and death, blessing and curse; therefore choose life, that you and your descendants may live" (Deut. 30:19).

And so whether he realizes it or not, in identifying some of the decisive choices that have given contour to his new character, this unorthodox crypto-Catholic has in fact relied on four tried and true tenets of his native Catholicism in its purest and simplest iteration. In his deepened relations with others, he has rediscovered *koinōnia*, the holiness of human fellowship, which sustains us all. In casting aside the compulsion to lay blame, he has uncovered the liberating quality of *forgiveness*, which is the human manifestation of divine grace. In finding the seed of the good amid the mud of the bad, he has realized the sublime worth of *redemption*, which allows all of us not to justify suffering but to utilize it if, in his words, we choose to take advantage.

Finally, in placing such a premium on *choice* itself, he is underscoring the idea first suggested in Eden's sylvan glen that our relationship with God is volitional: we either choose to enter into it, or we choose to reject it. In what Don refers to as the choices that shape our eternal character, we can hear echoes of old orthodoxy, claiming that every decision we make either draws us to God or drifts us away. Don's theology is a variation on the James Lowell hymn that proclaims, "Once to every life and nation, comes the moment to decide, / In the strife of truth with falsehood, for the good or evil side." From where Don sits, though, it is not just once that we decide. Rather, we are deciding lifelong, either building or dismantling our character, brick by brick.

Fellowship, forgiveness, redemption, volition. Whether arrived at in a straight-arrow line of Christian doctrine or with side trips through the lands of Buddha's Kapilavastu, the Stoic Zeno's Greece, or the hidden lairs of the Taliban, what Don has found for himself is very much what all people of faith pine for as we wonder, if not *why* we are here, then what it is that will give enduring value to the fact *that* we are here.

## WHENCE IMMORTALITY?

At the risk of psychologizing another man's faith, I can't help but wonder how Don's belief in the immortality of his character has been influenced by his life experiences. By his own reckoning, he lost his identity from the attack in 2003. The house, as he put it, was already burned to the ground. Is the immortality of what he calls "character" at root an effort to strap a flak jacket on to his newly emergent identity? Make it impervious to further attack? Put another way, does his need for security dictate the contours of the belief? Or do the contours of the belief simply make security a welcomed derivative? Which is the chicken and which is the egg?

I cannot answer these questions and can only rely on my own observation that Don's beliefs are sincere, deeply held, and the product of a great deal of study and introspection, which is more than I can say for good many of us. What's more, all else being equal, I'll put my money on a theology that is grounded in life's experiences over one that is divorced from them. Boots on the ground trump heads in the clouds. Even if his belief in the durability of character is rooted in an existential *need* to believe in its durability, it is yet another example of the kind of adaptation this courageous man has made in the interest of maintaining some modicum of spiritual equilibrium.

## PERSEVERING

It comes as no surprise that over the next seven years post-injury, equilibrium has been both hard to grasp and even harder to keep. Much of what happened in the first months after the injury, in what Don now refers to as his "infancy," are lost to memory. His mother died in 2003, and when his father would come to visit him in rehab, he had to constantly remind Don that she was gone. His wife, holding no illusions that the "old Don" would ever return, eventually filed for divorce, an occurrence that, while leaving Don bereft, did not leave him embittered. "Unfortunately," as he points out, "I've seen [our] story played out countless times, and I have come to learn not to place judgment on the partners who leave." His sentiment is suggestive of one of those instances in his life where the by-product of magnanimity is serenity. If blame is unproductive, forgiveness yields sublime reward.

Like a lot of erstwhile rebellious sons, Don's relationship with his father has been punctuated by tender times and times when they've knocked the pins out from under one another. "My dad and I have irreconcilably different personalities," he tells me, "so the smartest move we've made has been to accept the differences rather than try to reconcile them." Their decision is reminiscent of the old Buddhist observation that you can't push a chain up a hill. Nevertheless, every once in a while, they seem to try to give the chain a shove.

"We're good together for about three or four days straight, after which we're just looking for trouble," he confesses. Then he goes on to relate a cautionary tale of how he, his dad, and his daughter took a fishing and hiking trip together to Alaska that, due to circumstances beyond their control, ran longer that the time they'd allotted.

"We were on a glacier, my dad and I on one side and my daughter clear on the other. There had been some meltdowns between my father and myself, and on this occasion I exceeded my threshold and let loose on my dad with every epithet I had learned in nineteen years of active duty as a United States Marine. After it passed, when I returned to my daughter, who was far enough away that she was practically in a different time zone, she had this stunned look on her face." He looks down, smiles, pauses for a good long time, then looks back up at me. "It turns out that there are great acoustics on a glacier." Nonetheless, the purge was good for them, a sort of cleansing flush that bought Don and his dad another few days of peace.

For any survivor of TBI, peace can be a tenuous thing, easily disrupted by a lost thought, a renegade emotion, or as Don points out, the unintended input of a misguided public. Perhaps his most persistent struggle, one he suspects will be with him until the day he achieves that immortality of character, is what he calls "being a red among the blue," the "red" as the community of TBI survivors, the "blue" as the other 99.9 percent of the world.

"Each day I put on my blue clothes and blue face paint and try to pass as blue because it is their world that I and others have to live in. By passing as blue, I can avoid others' pitying me, offering the kind of help I don't want, or making assumptions that are incorrect." This charade has its obvious advantages, but carries its risks as well.

He offers me this example: "I'm standing in front of the cashier at a local grocery store, and people are waiting behind me. I'm struggling to come up with the right change for the cashier, but I'm having a hard time of it. People behind me are getting restless, impatient. A young girl whispers something to her mother, who answers her in a theatrical whisper by saying to the little girl, 'Shhh . . . that poor man's retarded.'" He doesn't say so, but the contemptuous expression on his face tells me he is deeply bothered not only by the woman's condescending stupidity but also, like secondhand smoke, by her willingness to infect her daughter with it as well.

This is but one of a string of indignities that he and other reds suffer, that he must somehow learn how to interpret in light of the character he wishes to form for himself. There are others, perhaps none so poignant as the observation he makes about the nature of his wounds in the eyes of others: "It may sound petty, but imagine two wounded warriors walking down the street. One has a prosthetic limb, the other TBI. The civilian who spots the guy with the prosthesis is going to go out of his way to come over to that guy and thank him for serving his country. That same civilian is also going to go out of his way to avoid having to walk by the guy with TBI because the sight of us makes him uncomfortable. I can't tell you how many reds have told me essentially the same story."

## THRIVING

Indignities born of ignorance notwithstanding, the life of the new Don is a rich one that he eagerly rises each day to meet. His willingness to become more emotionally forthcoming has created new friendships and deepened old ones, first among them the one with his daughter. He used to treat this young woman like an older child and, had it not been for the TBI and his "new awakening," would probably be guilty of repeating the same sin. As he puts it, "she likes this version better." He also shares a profound bond with other TBI survivors, particularly those who have suffered war injuries. "We reds among the blues can often spot each other," he points out. "The brotherhood can be very strong, particularly because of the 'other' status that we feel." It is strong and, I am given to believe, it is strengthening; another form of that koinonia he so deeply cherishes.

He is also not without mission. In recent months he has tried to educate others as to the myriad unnecessary humiliations and hassles faced by wounded vets and others when they travel. "Plates in the skull, shrapnel, prosthetics, all make for a 100 percent likelihood that when you're traveling through an airport, you're going to be subjected to an enhanced pat-down. The same is true for elderly Americans, with artificial joints, pacemakers, and the like. These are two segments of the population that by all means shouldn't be singled out for pat-downs, so I'm trying to change this." At my first listen, it strikes me like a rather narrow cause to attach to. But then I consider that for the guy who's raising the issue, these pat-downs are literally adding insult to injury. My failure to pick this up at first blush is indicative of the luxury I enjoy—good fortune misconstrued as entitlement—of being a blue. I am like a guy whose biggest concern is whether or not the Mets will get their game in despite foreboding weather; it is my narrowness, not his.

When we are done talking, I am left wondering if in fact Don got to the fire too late. Or, if his abode burned down, is it possible that the house has been rebuilt? If it were all in jeopardy of being lost today, might the new Don want to lay hold of the therapist's advice to create of himself whomever he wanted to be? Or if not that, might he want to rescue his power to choose, so fundamental in the shaping of his character? I hint at this, and he gently chides me with this bit of wisdom, delivered with a sly smile: "Keep in mind that I'm only seven years old."

At my visit in 2010, it has been only seven years since the injury, and only five since he started reconstructing his sense of self. I realize that my nudging him is illustrative of my impertinence, just as his reserve is indicative of his patience. It is the Stoic in him. "Have patience with all things, but chiefly, have patience with yourself." So said Francis de Sales. Don understands that he is very much a work in progress, so at five years out, he is in no hurry to anoint one thing of greater value than another. Much like the way we started our conversation, I am trying to hurry him, yet he is coaxing me to move at his pace. He knows what is best for him. And for this, I salute him.

## Questions for Discussion

1. At one point Don states: "I'm much more precise now in understanding why I'm here. I am here to develop the character that I will take with me in my immortal life beyond this physical universe." What is the relationship (if any) between our actions in this life and eternity?

2. Don talks about the pivotal role that choices play in our lives. He sees them as a basic component of human character. Discuss this in light of the choice that was put before him by his speech therapist to "define" himself "any way he wants."

3. Why, in Don's understanding, is blame such a pointless exercise? Is this something you find difficult to relinquish?

# Chapter 13

# BRENDA BERKMAN

*Blessed Are . . .*

*I have an insatiable appetite to right wrongs.*
*It's probably some deep-seated Christian guilt!*
—Brenda Berkman

"YOU WANT TO KNOW WHAT I'D RESCUE FROM MY BURNING building?" asks Brenda Berkman, who then answers me with a candor that I would later come to recognize as characteristic of a woman of point-blank forthrightness in an age of the hedged bet and the weighed word.

"I would save the Beatitudes of Jesus Christ," she tells me, a tone of near defiance in her voice, as if she were accepting a dare, "and I'll tell you why."

"Please do," I ask, and as I hear what she then has to say, I get the distinct impression that this is a question whose answer Brenda has not conjured up but has lived into.

"Because I'd rather see the world as it could be than as it is, and if I'm reading them right, so did Jesus." She doesn't miss a beat. "When he blessed the hungry, he was acknowledging the existence of hunger. When he blessed the persecuted, he was acknowledging persecution. In each one of these passages, he was telling us how things are, which isn't so swell, but also

181

how things could be, which is a whole lot better. It's simple, really. I'd pull the Beatitudes out of the flames."

This directness befits Brenda. When you first meet her, you can't help but be struck her lack of adornment or excess. Denim jeans and a work shirt. Close-cropped salt-and-pepper air-dried hair and no makeup. Short of stature but trim and taut, she sits ramrod straight in her chair. Her arms are like thin-cabled steel, and she could not have so much as an ounce of excess fat on her body. Her eyes are riveting, as though when she looks at you she can stare halfway to your soul. Her features, which at first seem severe—single cocked eyebrow, pursed lips—soften considerably when she smiles. She's one of those people who smiles with their entire face, like a fist unclenching to reveal a gift in the palm of the hand.

And when it comes to both seeing the world as it could be and extinguishing flames in the hopes of rescuing those things that are most precious to us, Brenda speaks with the authority of wisdom born amid the ordeals of experience. Not only did she serve as a professional firefighter for over twenty years; she also was the first woman hired by the Fire Department of New York (FDNY). This appointment came only at the end of a protracted legal battle with an agency reluctant (to put it charitably) to ever see women crack the hallowed ranks of "New York's Bravest" (their motto). Now in her midfifties and in retirement, Brenda looks back on her desire to join the force and her struggle to make it happen; in both, she sees the message of the Beatitudes embodied in word and deed. My suspicion is right, I think: her words are not conjured up. Quite the opposite. They are deeply embedded.

"There were two reasons why I wanted to serve in the FDNY, and the first is pretty straightforward: I like the work. I like work that entails using both my body (my strength) and my wits (my mind). And firefighting demands both. When I worked in an office, which I did for some years, I had to think a lot, but I did it mostly on my ass, if you'll excuse my language."

But it's the second reason that really begins to get to the core of her values. "I very much wanted to do something that served the community," she tells me. "The fact of the matter is, when people are in their most desperate moments, when they don't know who else to call, they call us. And we never turn anybody down. We go into the poorest neighborhoods, the most dangerous situations, often with our own lives at risk, and we help people. I would often feel at my worst when we'd fight a fire in a home where the people clearly didn't have much to begin with. You'd look around and know that these folks didn't have insurance, didn't have bank accounts, didn't have access to a hotel. And whatever they *did* have was now gone, up in smoke."

As she says this, now a few years removed from active duty, a hint of sadness is still discernible in her voice and visage. She no longer serves this population as a firefighter, but it is clear to me that she continues to care deeply for them since her conversation is all in the present tense. Her musing then circles her back to the Beatitudes:

"When you talk about seeing the difference between how the world is and how it should be, nobody feels that distinction quite like a poor family that's just lost to fire what little they have, and in many instances someone they love." *"Blessed are the poor in spirit, for theirs is the kingdom of heaven"* (Matt. 5:3, emphasis added).

Brenda sums up her beliefs with characteristic succinctness leavened by a dose of modesty that truly becomes her: "I saw too much suffering in the world. I've always wanted to alleviate what I could alleviate. That's at the core of what Jesus taught, and it's at the core of how I want to live. I'm not saying I do a very good job of it, but it's how I *want* to live." *"Blessed are those who hunger and thirst for righteousness, for they shall be satisfied"* (Matt. 5:6, emphasis added).

But if she sees her vocation as one of transforming some small portion of the world into what it could be, it may be because Brenda has not been immune to experiencing the worst aspects of the world as it is. Her road from the court-house to the firehouse was not a smooth one, nor did life get much better once she'd arrived.

## BREAKING DOWN THE DOOR

It was 1978, a time when, in the irreverent words of one male firefighter I spoke with (who wished to remain anonymous), "one prerequisite to serving in the New York fire department was the ability to write your name in the snow." In that year Brenda initiated what would become a four-year lawsuit to overturn the all-male policy. Herself an attorney, a good many detractors dismissed her suit as a publicity stunt. "Why," they asked, "would anybody in their right mind pursue a job that was twice as challenging and half as lucrative as the one they currently hold?" Others rendered even harsher opinions, branding her a reckless, angry, headline-grabbing, agenda-driven feminist (as though feminism in and of itself was some-how pejorative) whose presence on the force would imperil the lives of the men she would be working alongside of and the citizens she'd be sworn to save.

She prevailed, but in many ways it was a Pyrrhic victory. Brenda was among a small group of women in her graduating class of firefighters, all of whom experienced indignities that went beyond what some male firefighters benignly referred to as "fraternal hazing." One female had a canister of tear gas tossed into the firehouse kitchen when she was preparing a meal. Another had a tombstone with her name engraved on it delivered to her door. More than one woman had the tires on her car slashed, air bled out of her oxygen tanks, dead rodents stuffed in her work boots, and as one might expect, a persistent silent treatment from the men who were supposed to be their comrades-in-arms. Many were victims of physical assault, and many others—Brenda included—the victims of sexual assault. It was not an easy go of it. Yet despite the hostile atmosphere, Brenda cherished the work she did with the FDNY, if not always the people with whom she did it. *"Blessed are those who are persecuted for righteousness' sake, for theirs is the kingdom of heaven"* (Matt. 5:10, emphasis added).

For all of the obstacles thrown in her path, Brenda not only endured, she also excelled. In 1994 she was promoted to lieutenant, and in 1996 became the first firefighter in America to serve as a White House Fellow, doing so in the office of the Secretary of Labor. In 2006, when she retired from the fire department after twenty-five years on the force, she did so at the rank of Captain. Some publicity stunt! She never returned to the practice of law.

Nonetheless, her focus is not on her own accomplishments—it never has been—but on that broader, beatific picture, the world as it could be. And when I ask her to reflect on how women fare in the department today as opposed to when she first joined the ranks, the look on her face becomes furtive, pensive, and longing, all at the same time.

"One way to look at that question is to talk about 9/11," she says, in a hush that can only be described as reverent. "Then let's talk about what happened in the weeks and months that followed. It's emblematic, I think, of how things are," as opposed, she implied, to how they should be. And so her tale began. . . .

## HEROES ALL

"September the 11th was supposed to be a day off for me, to the extent that firefighters ever have a real day off. It was primary day in New York, so I'd planned to do some campaigning for a candidate I was supporting. But shortly before I headed out the door to do just that, I got the phone call.

"My [firehouse] company is in Chelsea [a Manhattan neighborhood about a mile and a half from the towers], so there was no way I was going to make it down there to suit up and get equipped. Instead, I headed over to my old Brooklyn firehouse, not far from where I live, and joined the firefighters there. It was at a little after 10:00 in the morning when we got to what people now call Ground Zero. The second tower had just fallen; everything was a mess."

From here, Brenda tells a tale of Dante's first circle of hell: blazing heat and blinding smoke, mass confusion and system-wide communications breakdowns, whole fire companies unaccounted for, and passing moments of great relief when someone, *any*one was spotted alive. "I kept looking for 12 Truck [her command] but never found them" (by which she means she found the vehicle but not the firefighters who came down to the Trade Center on it). "In the end, all I could do was keep the guys immediately around me, the guys from the Brooklyn house, as safe as possible."

She did this—she kept them working and kept them safe—but that feat offered little consolation when she later learned that of the 343 firefighters who lost their lives that day, three of them were from 12 Truck, all of whom had died even before she'd arrived. In fact, in assessing the loss some months later, Brenda did the math and figured out that throughout the length of her career, she had, at one time or another, worked with 250 of those 343.

At midnight that night she went home, bone-weary, fourteen hours after arriving. With many of her colleagues, she returned the next day and nearly every day thereafter over the next six weeks, sifting the rubble, looking for comrades, and extinguishing some of the ancillary fires that ignited long after the initial blast. "I remember the shifting steel cutting into my hands as we moved the debris. I remember fires burning for up to six months after the initial blast. One day I was hit by a truck. And all the while we're sucking God-knows-what down into our lungs."

When I ask Brenda about some of the feelings that attend her memories of that experience, it is clear that this is something she's pondered often in the nine years since 9/11; she is as quick with an answer as she is sure of its content.

"At first," she tells me, "there was this extraordinary bond among firefighters, forged by our grief. None of the differences that might've one time driven us apart could keep us apart. Lots of hugging, lots of tears." Then, after a long pause and a downward gaze, she adds. "Lots of funerals."

But the goodwill was more a flicker than an eternal flame. "Even before the last of our comrades was laid to rest, I began feeling the sting of discrimination that has been a part of every woman's tenure—my own included—on the force.

"I particularly remember an incident that happened when I attended the funeral for Fr. Mychal Judge [Chaplain to the fire department and one of the first casualties of 9/11]. I considered Mychal a dear friend and a real confidant, and I was more than a little broken up the day we buried him. So it just added to my grief that morning when a retired firefighter—a male, a real crusty old-timer—came up to me, *at the funeral*, looked me square in the eye, and said, 'I wish the towers had fallen on you instead.' I can't tell you how deeply that hurts: a real dagger in the heart. *"Blessed are you when men revile you and persecute you and utter all kinds of evil against you . . ."* (Matt. 5:11, emphasis added).

## THE WEAKER SEX?

"It may seem a petty complaint to the outsider, but the fact is, in the aftermath of 9/11 the uniformed women were once again treated like non-entities, like we didn't exist. What really hurt me was that this was typical of how we were often treated on the force. Even 9/11, even this defining event for every single firefighter in the FDNY, didn't heal that. In every speech, every press release, every sound bite, every eulogy—or so it seemed—it was the *men* who were remembered, the *men* who were heroes, the *men* who were cited for their bravery and heroism. None of us doubt the men's heroism, not for a moment. But although there were only twenty women on the fire department force at the time, all of them were there too, and all of them did their part. And beyond us were women EMTs (emergency medical technicians), women transit authority cops, women NYPD officers."

Brenda then begins a short litany, precise as though it were rehearsed. Her tempo quickens, and she leans into her words as she leans into her audience, ticking off names on her fingers, one by one:

"Kathy Mazza, a port authority police captain, died in the line of duty that day. So did an EMT by the name of Yamel Merino. Moira Smith, a New York City police officer, was photographed while leading somebody out of one of the towers. Immediately after she got him to safety, she went back inside and was in there when the building collapsed. These are forgotten names." There is more than a trace of righteous indignation in her voice, as righteous as it is indignant, and pain as pure as if it were newfound rather than years old.

## MILES TO GO

One of the reasons Brenda is so wounded by the neglect shown the women in uniform has to do with how she came to be a firefighter in the first place. As a child of the Midwest, growing up in the 1950s and '60s, she'd received a steady drumbeat of messages underscoring the notion that the all-boys club was as prevalent as it was impenetrable, that there were certain venues in this world beyond writing your name in the snow that held no place for women and never would.

"In those days [of my youth] we might just as well have been invisible. When I was a kid, I had a wicked fastball and a real passion for baseball, but these were pre-Title IX days. So when my mom tried to sign me up for Little League, we were told it was 'boys only.' Later, in school, when I demonstrated a proficiency in math, I remember my guidance counselor telling me that girls are supposed to be better in English, so I should direct my studies accordingly. The way I read that, I was being discouraged from pursuing studies that might take me into, say, the hard sciences and directed instead toward the humanities. Poetry instead of physics.

"Later still, when I was in college, female lawyers were still almost unheard of. When I applied to law school, women were just starting to enter the legal field in any real numbers. So don't think for a minute that in a profession as fundamentally conservative as law there weren't subtle tyrannies imposed by a legal system that had been run largely by men for over two hundred years. It was very tough to be taken seriously."

Brenda's plaints recalled to mind a trenchant observation of the nineteenth-century educator and author Elizabeth Missing Sewell: "Boys are sent out into the world to buffet with its temptations, to mingle with bad and good, to govern and direct—girls are to dwell in quiet homes among few friends, to exercise a noiseless influence." But Brenda's influence was destined to be something other than noiseless.

"Needless to say, when I made the decision to become a firefighter," she continued, "I was by no means deaf to the echoes in my head telling me, yet again, that the absence of a Y chromosome was going to keep me from following my dream. So twenty years later, after having prevailed in that dream, after believing that I could take this one little piece of the world as it is and help change it into what it could be, and standing much closer to the end of my career than the onset, the message I got was that very little ground had been broken and very little change had been made. Uniformed women, even those who bore the sufferings and sacrifices of 9/11, were still invisible." Not only that, she adds, as if as a postmortem, "thirty years out there are fewer women in the FDNY than were in my graduating class."

## BLESSED ARE THOSE WHO MAKE PEACE WITH THEMSELVES

I consider the sweep of Brenda's life thus far and can't help but wonder if she's being too hard on herself in her insistence that when it comes to the matter of the redress of discrimination, her labors have been mightier than the results they've yielded. It is as though she works under the assumption that if prejudices long sustained aren't quickly felled, it's indicative of a failure of will on the part of David rather than entrenched self-interest on the part of Goliath. Perhaps, I think, she fails to take into account the extent to which beneficiaries of injustice are, by nature, saboteurs of change. When I ask her about this, she cracks a coy, inscrutable smile and cops to a holy impatience that has long been a part of her makeup.

"I have an insatiable appetite to right wrongs, no doubt a part of some deep-seated Christian guilt that I harbor," she tells me, only half kidding. "The truth be told, I was raised in a religious household, but I only went to church to make my parents happy. I got my Christianity driven into me from the time I was a young child, but the sense of joy that religion is supposed to deliver wasn't as strong as the sense of obligation it was supposed to induce." I remind her of a line from H. L. Mencken to the effect that Puritanism is "the haunting fear that someone, somewhere, is having a good time." Her smile widens, and she nods in agreement.

That said, she goes on to acknowledge that she is constitutionally ill-suited to that piece of the religious puzzle that extols the merits of inner peace as much as it esteems the morality of social justice. "I'm afraid I'd make a lousy Buddhist," she tells me. "I'm not very Zen, I don't have a lot of peace inside of me. It's not very Christlike, but I find I have very little tolerance for people who don't make an effort to make the world a better place." I hear this as a sort of confession, the difference between how her own comportment is and how she would like it to be. It is the beatitudes writ small and very, very personal. Some of the world's pain that she wants so desperately to alleviate is contained within her own soul.

She continues with her self-assessment. "I frankly would like to be more Christlike in that regard; more understanding and tolerant of folks who don't necessarily have the same passion for justice that I see in myself."

So with this appraisal, it seems only natural that we turn our attention back to the Beatitudes, in particular about how the merciful will obtain mercy (Matt. 5:7). One of us is reminded of an observation attributed to Thomas Jefferson, about how the Bible can sometimes be experienced as an echo chamber. Shout into it, "I demand justice!" and in return you're likely to hear God's voice saying, "*I* demand justice!" right back to you. On the other hand, if you plead "Mercy?" you're just as likely to hear back "Mercy!"

"My anger may have gotten the better of me in those last, post 9/11 years with the [fire] department," she goes on. "I think about the discrimination I felt in my own life and saw in the lives of others, and sometimes it really got to me. The world as it was. When I spoke earlier about how devastating it was for me to go into the burning homes of poor people and see them lose the little they had with no real recourse, that was mostly confined to my work as a firefighter. But after 9/11 I began to see it elsewhere; in the television scenes of bombed-out schools in Baghdad, then in the poorest neighborhoods of New Orleans (after Katrina in 2005), then most recently in Haiti (after the 2010 earthquake).

"To be perfectly honest with you, I was rather much perpetually angry, burned out, exhausted, and frustrated. I wasn't driven by love, which meant that no matter how faithfully I tried to live up to the Beatitudes, I wasn't being very Christlike. It was time to go."

And so she did. Having begun her career as an unwanted, unwelcome, marginalized, and lowly cadet, Brenda Berkman retired twenty-five years later as a Captain in the FDNY, a leader of men (and a few women).

## DOORS CLOSE, DOORS OPEN

Retirement has neither slowed her pace nor slaked her thirst to breathe life into beatitudes that she loves so dearly, nor has it necessarily instilled in her the patience and inner peace she has longed for during much of her adult life. But it has helped her make some progress.

"When I left the department, I wanted to find a way to continue to be of service to the poor," she begins. "So I hooked up with a church [Fifth Avenue Presbyterian, in the heart of Manhattan] that had this fabulous outreach to people in need, particularly New York's swelling homeless population. I started by volunteering in the food program, 'Meals on Heels.' Then a funny thing started to happen.

"The more time I spent at the kitchen, the more contact and conversation I started to have with the church's parishioners who were also volunteering. We became our own little community, our own fellowship. So that led me to drop by on the occasional Sunday, make myself as inconspicuous as possible, and listen, if only with one ear—I still considered myself a pretty committed agnostic at the time—to the morning's sermon."

From here, Brenda paints a picture of her courtship with the church as a kind of slow-moving minuet between an eager suitor and his reluctant prospect. Wary of the hidebound institutional conservatism that can sometimes choke the lifeblood out of a church, she did not want to become a part of any organization that would look to dampen her iconoclastic spirit or ply her with platitudes that reduce the troubles of the world to the indecipherable ways of an inscrutable God. Over time, she was not disappointed.

"I met people like me, and that was good. But I also met people not at all like me, and that was even better. I found myself in this community of diversity and inclusiveness, rich and poor, black and white, gay and straight; some folks educated on the campuses of great universities, some educated on the streets, some not educated at all. Left of center, right of center. Dead center!

"Just as important, though," she continues, "the sermons were really speaking to me. They made me think, made me examine some of my long-held beliefs and question some of my biases, helped to strengthen my resolve about trying to make the world a better place, and just as important, to bring a little peace to myself."

I ask her if this church doesn't perhaps represent—in microcosm and by no means perfectly—the world as it could be. She sits back, considering the question.

"It does. But we don't live there; we simply congregate there," she tells me. "It's a lot easier to model that behavior within those walls for a few sacred hours. The real challenge is taking it *beyond* those walls." She pauses again, deep in thought, and then adds, with a glint in her eye, "But that's not only the challenge; that's also the fun."

Asked about other outlets for her energies and passions, she names two. "First, I volunteer pretty regularly down at Ground Zero, with the 9/11 Families' Association Tribute Center, giving tours to people and interpreting to them both what happened and what is happening there now." (This interview was conducted when Ground Zero was largely a construction site and no memorial was yet in existence.) "In the spirit of trying to live a more loving life, I try to take great care with what I say, and I conclude every tour by telling the people that I hope they've heard something from me that will allow them to take a little love back to their communities."

"Why," I ask her, "do you end your tours this way?"

"Because it's easy to come away angry at what happened there, as though there are still smoldering embers buried in those grounds waiting to be reignited. And that doesn't do anybody any good. We need to find love in this place that was destroyed by hate."

"All hatred driven hence, the soul recovers . . . innocence," wrote Yeats, and I cannot think of a more apt example of "hatred driven hence," of taking the world as it is and turning it on its head, into what it should be, than Brenda's witness at the scene of this horrific crime. The Beatitudes live. They live at Ground Zero, in New York City. They live there because FDNY Capt. Brenda Berkman, who lost 343 of her colleagues there, sees to it that they live.

"Is it ever difficult for you?" I ask her, and she answers by recounting a story for me.

"Do you remember how I told you that when I got to the site on 9/11, I couldn't find my company's truck [Ladder 12]?"

"I do," I tell her.

"Well, one day, not all that long ago, a select group of us were invited to tour an airplane hangar that contained a lot of the rubble from the World Trade Center. We get off the bus and go inside, and I'm in the midst of this huge building with broken, twisted pieces as far as my eye can see. I start walking down one of the aisles, and I turn a corner. And there it is!" She pauses a moment, a clutch in her throat and inexpressible pain etched across her face. "Ladder 3. Crushed. Ladder 3 was a company down the street from me. I knew and worked with the firefighters who had ridden to the Trade Center on that truck, including some of my friends." Upon laying eyes on it, she burst into tears.

I watch Brenda wrestle with her grief, for this is what she does. She does not let it wash over her; instead, ever poised, she tries to beat it back as if fearful that if she doesn't will it away, it will threaten to overwhelm her. I can't help but wonder if what I'm seeing isn't somehow connected to her crusade for the women of Ground Zero to get the recognition they deserve and have been denied. Perhaps when she takes up the cause of the forgotten women, it is not just a matter of gender equality, of acknowledging the contributions made by women in uniform at Ground Zero and anywhere they willfully put themselves in harm's way for the sake and safety of the rest of us. Perhaps when Brenda gives voice to the disquiet in her soul, it is not just grounded in this issue but is also part of a deeper and more profound disquiet that can't be measured by numbers or silenced by a belated honoring of those otherwise forgotten.

Perhaps, I think to myself, it is safer for her, as it is for all of us, to sublimate inconsolable pain by transforming it into a worthy cause because, while the pain renders us utterly helpless, we are at least left with some power to exert over the cause. Rage and tears are so easily intermixed—indeed, rarely does anger exist without sadness or vice versa—that this affords us the opportunity at least to mitigate that helplessness if not overcome it. Such behavior is a two-edged sword, though; it's redemptive insofar as it creates some good out of an otherwise dreadful situation, but it also runs the risk of allowing us to suppress our pain in the mistaken belief that by doing so we've conquered it. Only later, when it surfaces in odd and sometimes unidentifiable guise, do we get the first hint that it is in a position to conquer *us*.

Perhaps too, this is what has enticed Brenda to the other outlet for her passions: she makes art. Her medium is lithographic print, and her subjects are quite everyday things, approachable objects in simple and uncluttered display, graspable to an eye as untrained as mine. One, which she calls "Hide and Seek," is a whimsical Modigliani-like rendering of two goldfish oblivious to one another amid a swirl of kelp, while another, titled "Absence Makes the Heart," depicts a solitary figure at a dusk-gray seashore and seems reminiscent of the lonely moods of Edward Hopper or Andrew Wyeth. Yet another, "Jump," a rendering of the old parachute ride at Coney Island, has an appropriately light-as-air and free-falling quality to it and could hang in a child's nursery. Brenda seems to gravitate toward random subjects alike in their ordinariness, eliciting eclectic moods and perhaps bearing witness to an artist still in search of her own signature style.

Though the moods vary, the overall feel I come away with when I look at her work is that if it is not the product of a woman fully at peace with herself, what peace she does find is enhanced when she has an artist's pencil in her hand. It seems clear to me that her art is no less important to her, no less restorative to her, than her volunteer work or her commitment to her causes.

For years now, Brenda has done the deeds of the saint. The lonely, quixotic, often misconstrued or ill-received work of doing as the Beatitudes encourage her to do, it is the task of reassembling the broken pieces of a fallen world. And while that passion, that fire, continues to burn white-hot within her, it seems as though she has of late taken on a task even more daunting and more courageous. For now she also goes about the business of internalizing these biblical verses that mean the world to her. As she does so, she seems to understand that there are times when the reservoir of anger we hold for others is indicative of a paucity of love we hold for ourselves, and that Jefferson's mandate may be the wisest of all. Ask for mercy, receive mercy, bestow mercy. On ourselves, as well as on others.

❧

There's a saying common in AA meetings. Recovering alcoholics and drug addicts will often tell newcomers to the group to "fake it till you make it."

What they mean by this is that people new to recovery have to behave in a manner that suggests they're committed to sobriety even if their yearnings are still pulling them in another, more destructive direction. The thinking here is that in time their convictions will catch up with their behavior; comport yourself like you want to remain dry, and in time you will in fact *want* to remain dry. Like so much about AA, it is pure common sense; healthy behavior is self-reinforcing, and reinforced behavior buttresses the feelings we attach to that behavior. The longer alcoholics remains sober, the longer they want to remain sober and therefore the more compellingly they believe in sobriety. There's an element of this thinking that applies to Brenda's fealty to the Beatitudes; indeed, at various points in our own lives, I am quite certain it applies to all of us.

Brenda's conviction is to live a life compatible with these monumental moral gems—no one ever accused her of setting her sights low—but by her own admission the deeds come more easily than the sentiments behind them. She does the things that make for peace but doesn't necessarily feel the peace herself. Driven by her own history of feeling disregarded, she does loving things for people who have similarly suffered such disregard; yet she is driven more by the anger she holds for the perpetrators of that suffering than by the love she holds for its bearers. Her compassion for the poor is great but perhaps not as great as her disdain for a culture that allows poverty to exist alongside extravagant wealth. While she harnesses that disdain to do good things, she is right to want love to prevail over resentment. It is simply better for her soul. And after all, what is it but love that undergirds the Beatitudes, that gives them their durability and moral heft? And who among us has never done a noble thing with less than noble feelings in our hearts?

But if Brenda is fakin' it till she makes it, she may well be inching closer to making it all the time. She started out helping at the church meals program but remaining on the periphery, only to find herself slowly drawn in, first to the church's social service community and eventually to the church community as a whole. Good deeds are giving rise to a sense of fellowship in a loving community.

Her journey is all of ours, not once and for all, but in all places and at all times. It is the journey of head and heart, of knowing how to do right and learning how to *be* right, until such time that, every so often in a moment of true grace, rightness is not external to us but wells up from deep within and comes forth in irresistible gesture. It is the kind of moment that, in Brenda's words, "turns the world upside down."

## Questions for Discussion

1. What do the Beatitudes tell us about how the world can be, and by inference how the world is? Choose one beatitude and discuss it.
2. Berkman is quite open in this chapter about her own lack of peace, despite all the good works she does. Can peaceful actions lead to a peaceful life? Or does a peace-

ful life give rise to peaceful actions? What is the interplay between the two?

3. Have you ever had to overcome something as daunting as what Berkman faced when she wanted to join the fire department? If so, what did the experience do to either strengthen or sap your sense of hope in humankind?

# CONCLUSION

## *Confessions of a Guilty Bystander*

*Differences challenge assumptions.*
—Anne Wilson Schaef

ONE OF THE RAPS AGAINST SHRINKS (AS WELL AS CLERGY) IS that while we're licensed to tease out the juiciest nuggets about other people's lives, we don't divulge so much as the skimpiest morsels of our own. We simultaneously hold our cards close to the vest and insist that persons on the other side of the table lay theirs down for uncensored inspection. I might know that the reason a patient or parishioner has a penchant for cocaine cocktails is because he was physically abused for the better part of his childhood by a miscreant uncle, but he doesn't know so much as my favorite book, play, or restaurant.

The reason this beef has some legs to it is because even though the practice of rigorous one-way revelation is indispensable to the therapeutic relationship, more than a few of us go into this line of work in part *because* we're disposed to self-secrecy. It's a part of our character. For whatever constellation of reasons (and wherever those reasons fall on the neurotic ↔ healthy spectrum), we are loathe to have others know what it is in our makeup that triggers a quick smile or a slow burn, what makes us tick or ticks us off, what stirs our heart or roils our gut, maybe even what our favorite restaurant is. So we avoid the issue by choosing a line of work where nondisclosure is more mandate than proposition.

I say this because it came to bear on the writing of this book. Or more to the point, it bears on the conversations that surrounded the writing of it. When I mentioned to interested third parties what the gist of the book was going to be, it invariably led to parlor-game chatter about what they would rescue from the flames, and just as inevitably, questions about what *I* would rescue. I demurred as a matter of course, my rationale being that I wanted to canvass everyone else first, see what rich troves of insight my interviews yielded, and only then take a look at how those interviews shaped my own answer. It was a bit of a dodge that, as it turns out, had the added benefit of being true. And useful.

In the spirit of full disclosure, as happy as I would have been to avoid going public with the particulars of my own value system, I knew it would've been an indefensible and unmitigated act of cowardice to do so (not that I've ever proved myself incapable of such cowardice). I just can't ask of others what I wouldn't disclose of myself. But by waiting (okay, stalling) until I'd interviewed all the brave souls who agreed to participate in this project, I came to see how my own values have indeed been shaped and clarified by this process of discovery. What I come out with, and what I come out of the fire with, is this: I would rescue my appreciation for the richness and variegation that makes the human race as distinctive and, well, as flat-out fascinating as it is.

It is an idea with which I have had only passing acquaintance until now. I've always given intellectual nod to the diversity of our species; after all, we speak over 6,000 languages and reside in over 190 countries, where we live in mansions, capes, ranches, yurts, huts, tepees, caves, and homeless shelters. We venerate saints, statues, sacred cows, and peyote. We spend our free time at ball games, ballets, brothels, and bullfights. And so on; you get the idea. That said, I've never felt it in my bones, never truly *treasured* how much richer all of our lives are because of this variety. That is, until now.

Now, when I read the transcripts of the interviews that have found a path into this little book, I realize in a much more full-throated way how different each of us are as we set about the business of organizing and prioritizing our lives. Some of us do so with more intentionality than others; but for all of us, a great array of variables comes into play that yield an exponentially greater array of priorities. Our decision about what we would pull out of the fire is influenced by the particulars of our birth, the expectations of our culture, the limits of our intelligence, the richness of our imagination, the breadth of our opportunities, the scope of our means, the functionality of our family, and the crapshoot that is our DNA. And to this we could add that it is further influenced by whatever invisible forces of chance and accident, from a stray bullet to a winning lottery ticket, are hiding in the wings. And to *this* amalgam of forces we could further add both the extent to which we can control those forces and the extent to which they can control us. To put it briefly, the things we value and the extent to which we value them is very much a product of luck, work, choice, and circumstance, the end result being a cornucopia of possibility and a feast of differences.

## GENEROUS PEOPLE, THOUGHTFUL ANSWERS

When I think back to some of the interviews, beyond the diversity that was so much the coin of the realm, I am struck by two things: First, I was both impressed and grateful at how much thought each person gave to their response. Nobody spoke frivolously or carelessly; they brooded and pondered the question. There were lots of trenchant muses, furrowed brows, tented fingers, skyward gazes, and pensive pauses; their comments were reflective of the tremendous attention they paid to the art of puzzling out what it was they wanted to say and how they wanted to say it. It was as if they *valued* the exercise itself.

And second, I was captivated by the collective content of the answers they gave. Very few people identified physical possessions, and those who did so did not mention things of great material worth. Cathrine Kellison spoke of the box that held her journals (and her weed) because she was really talking about the memories she held dear as she faced the likelihood of her own death at an early age. Arthur Waskow identified his computer because he was really treasuring his writings, which are not just writings but are also windows onto his very heart. Alan Alda, whose career as an actor has been immensely rewarding to him, would rather preserve his understanding of reality and the heartache that sometimes accompanies it than any of the multitudinous material goods with which that career has rewarded him. What people value so highly—or at least what these people value—goes well beyond the wants and needs of the physical world and deep into the atmospherics of the soul.

## EVERYBODY'S GOT SOMETHING TO SAY

The idea for this book originated when my former editor, Stephanie Egnotovich, approached me with an observation and a question. "You know so many interesting people," she told me. (That's true insofar as I am far and away the most boring in the bunch. I'm the beige in a field of Technicolor.) "Why don't you interview some of them," she asked me, "and get them to talk about what it is in life that means the most to them?" I took the challenge, reworked it a bit, pitched it to a few of my friends, and they did the rest. The heavy lifting was all theirs.

Stephanie was right about one thing but perhaps a little off about another. She was correct to assume that people she found interesting and unusual would in turn have interesting things to say in response to the book's premise. But the mistake she may have made was in assuming that *only* people who have the kinds of life stories that jump out at you would be able to provide the depth of insight and opulence of thought she was looking for. Therefore this project brought unforeseen treasures for me and my readers.

The riches of the book were brought by the subjects of its component chapters, but the dividends of the experience were paid by the people I didn't interview (and in some cases people I didn't even know) who knew the book's premise, genially weighed in with their own take on the question, and displayed as much variety and imagination as did the people whose stories have been presented in these preceding pages.

I remember a peace corps worker who told me the thing she would want to hang on to is her sense of humility because without it she could not do her job for fear of her moral imperiousness getting the better of her. A recovering alcoholic twenty-two years sober told me he would rescue the "Serenity Prayer," the prayer most closely identified with Alcoholics Anonymous ("God, grant me the serenity to accept things I cannot change . . .") because it was the only prayer he could faithfully utter. Without it, he said, he would not be able to speak to God and would, he was quite certain, commit slow suicide at the narrow end of a Jack Daniel's bottle. I also spoke with a drug abuser, not in recovery, who told me the one thing he would pull from the fire is his amphetamines, because sometimes what we regard as our god is simply a wolf in sheep's clothing.

On a more optimistic note, I remember meeting a woman who spoke of her lust for knowledge because it kept her young. She was ninety-eight years old, and our conversation took place at a lecture on dialectical materialism. Perhaps my favorite, though, was the three-year-old boy playing in a sandbox with his buddies; when asked what meant the most in the world to him, he looked at me like I was an idiot and answered, somewhat curtly, "Sand." If I could have transformed his facial expression into words, it might come out something along the lines of "How can you be so obtuse?"

It was these and other people who reminded me that there are not only no duplicates; there are also no uninteresting people, not at the very core of our being. There are those I might not want to sit with at a cocktail party or on a cross-country bus ride because our stories and personalities would find no point of intersection, but maybe that's less a commentary on the narrowness of their lives than on the limits of my tolerance. More important, I came away from conversations both casual and formal with the distinct understanding that virtually no one lacks some sense, however articulate or inchoate, of what is of ultimate value to them.

## E PLURIBUS UNUM

What I also came away with is the realization that, in category if not in particular, those things that my interviewees revere are in turn, and in different measures, held in high regard by most everybody. For all of our variety, there is also kinship. What makes us akin is the fact that there are certain near universal truths we esteem; what makes us unique is that we all arrange those truths a little differently, seeing them with shades and nuance peculiar to us. We are like shuffled decks of playing cards: the component parts are much the same while the arrays and arrangements differ.

Thus while not everyone on earth will regard the painted canvas or the poetic word as highly as John Alexander or Mariah Britton respectively, I believe we all do have an appreciation of the aesthetic, of the value of beauty to the human heart, and of the worth of the artist whose calling it is to express that beauty in words that the heart can comprehend. Nor will all of us show the indefatigable optimism of Tao Porchon-Lynch. But by the same token, no one will question the power of hope embodied in her life story, and perhaps even the role that power has played in her longevity. Likewise for Don Lange and Chris Lim, who both spoke of a thirst for knowledge as indispensable to their emergent beings. Though not all of us will be as inquisitive, we can all agree on the great good that is evinced by the harnessing and harvesting of human intelligence, not to mention the corresponding ills that have been visited upon the earth as the by-product of our ignorance. The reluctant Presbyterian Brenda Berkman spoke of righting wrongs as eloquently as the devoutly Buddhist Kenjitsu Nakagaki did of the need for compassion, and both gave more than a passing nod to inner peace. In theological argot these qualities translate as justice and mercy, without which, in equal measure, humanity would have no basis for ethics.

In fact, in the eyes of the spiritually or religiously devout, theology infuses everything that was spoken of in these pages, because the best of what we are and the heights to which we aspire are in a sense incarnational. That is to say, it is the human embodiment of the divine intent. For what is it that God asks of us, as the prophet Micah (6:8) posed, but that we seek justice and mercy, beauty and truth? That we live with a sense of hope and an understanding of history? That we know both who we are and whose we are? Whether couched in the language of the religious or the secular, whether uttered by the believer, the skeptic, the agnostic, the indifferent or the evangelical atheist—the principles articulated by those who allowed themselves to be interviewed for this book are no less than sacred things.

## A JOYFUL NOISE

Perhaps then a deck of cards is too dry a metaphor for both the similarities that make us kin and the differences that define our uniqueness. Instead, what comes to mind is something more elegant. Think of music, for instance. There are only seven fundamental notes, yet those notes and their variants, when combined with the genius of the creator, have given us everything from Rachmaninoff's Études-Tableaux in E-flat Minor to Martin Luther's "A Mighty Fortress Is Our God"; from Ella Fitzgerald's "Oh, Lady Be Good!" to "Gin and Juice," by Calvin Cordozar Broadus Jr., aka Snoop Dogg.

Perhaps this is what we are. Sweet notes, joyful noises made of the same stuff and destined for the same end, but in the interim, sounding different enough to distinguish ourselves from others yet similar enough to be reminded that we are all children of the one who creates, redeems, and sustains us. "Amazing grace, how sweet the sound."

## Questions for Discussion

1. What would you pull from the fire? What are you leaving behind?
2. How does human diversity strengthen us? How does diversity invite impediments to our sense of community? What is the difference between diversity and inclusiveness?
3. What must we sacrifice of ourselves in order to coexist in a world of such varying opinions, beliefs, values, desires, and resources?

CPSIA information can be obtained at www.ICGtesting.com
Printed in the USA
BVOW01s2349230315

392967BV00001B/25/P